Sign Language
A Look at the Historic and Pro.

MW00479105

Great Thunder Publishing, Maricopa, Arizona

ISBN 978-0-9847706-0-1

Cover design by Mark Sequeira, MJA Studios
Email: mark@mjastudios.com

TABLE OF CONTENTS

ENDORSEMENTS

Terry Wildman is both loving and courageous in calling the church to "remove the log from our own eye" when it comes to America's history with its indigenous peoples. Who is more our neighbor we are called to love than those on whose land we all live and worship? With whom should we "first be reconciled" if not these peoples who have been so gravely mistreated on these shores? Who more should we become like in "all things" than those who cultures first gave meanings and ways of living to this place we now all share? Without bitterness or rancor, but with honesty and spiritual insight, Terry takes American Christians to places we all absolutely need to go.

(The Rev.) Russell Yee, Ph.D., California
Author of *Worship on the Way* (Judson Press)

My friends, Terry and Darlene Wildman, introduce readers to the mostly untold and shameful legacy of American national genocidal history against the first inhabitants of the land. They provide a major key to understanding this genocide by identifying the interconnectedness between Christian theology and imperial ideology. Together they issue a call to action to Christians to respond to this enduring injustice with the heart and lifestyle of restoration and redemption by helping create a new and better future. Not one born of guilt and shame, but mercy, repentance, forgiveness and love—notable signs of those who claim to follow Jesus. I hope you can hear the call!

Dr. Richard Twiss, D.Miss., Sicangu Lakota
Author of *One Church, Many Tribes*,
President, Wiconi International

In Sign Language Terry Wildman has written a powerfully truthful yet deeply compassionate treatise that shares a Biblical perspective to help us deal with a deep historical wound in the United States—that of the Church's relationship our own Native American People (and with Indigenous people around the world). Sadly the Church has often been silent and looked the other way in the face of gross injustice and even genocide. Even more tragic it has at times collaborated with the Government and other institutions in denying Native Americans love, value, dignity and justice while their peoples were being decimated, dislocated and deprived of the most basic of human rights. Terry is not attempting to "bash" the Church but is offering up a deep cry of Creator Father God's heart for reconciliation, forgiveness, justice and restoration. Terry gives us word pictures that deeply impact our hearts, language we can use to enter into a deep dialog with one another; and simple practical strategies to cross the divide of fear, hate and hurt and begin the healing process. If we listen and act upon this it will begin to lay the foundation of Revival & Reformation we so desperately need, are praying for and Jesus died for.

Ronald A. Archer, California
North American Coordinator
International Reconciliation Coalition

Thank you Terry for the prophetic challenge you have set before us in Sign Language. It deeply challenges me (and I trust others) regarding what my forefathers, the Puritans and Scotch-Irish, laid into the United States of America's foundations—a theology that could justify the removal of land and culture from the Native American peoples. May it indeed "bring understanding and insight into the history of this land so that we can see the present more clearly, and participate with God in those things that further his love and Kingdom."

"He who has an ear, let him hear what the Spirit is saying to the churches." Revelation 2:29.

Harry Smith, Northern Ireland
Author of *Heal Not Lightly*
Dignity Restored (www.dignityrestored.org)

Terry Wildman has been on a journey. Not only a journey of physical mobility as a musician, but also of pursuit of knowledge and revelation. Many folks across North America have come to appreciate Terry and his wife Darlene as RainSong, the talented award-winning singer-songwriters. But, Terry is more than that. He is a man of depth, compassion, and the pursuit of God's will for our days. He earnestly desires to learn from the past and to impart that knowledge into the present. As a Native American voice, my friend Terry has an affinity and appreciation for the mistreatment of the First Nations peoples of the Americas over hundreds of years. Sign Language is a compilation of Terry's journey to date. I recommend Terry and his book to you, knowing that some of what he has to say will be new information, and in some cases quite provocative. May this prophetic book open minds and hearts on behalf of the Almighty.

Thomas P. Dooley, Ph.D., Alabama
Author of *Hope When Everything Seems Hopeless*
Entrepreneur-Scientist and President of PathClearer Inc.
(www.pathclearer.com)

Sign Language carries thoughts that have needed to be expressed to the Body of Christ for many years. Within its pages Terry has boldly painted a picture of truth that exists between the Native American Indian and the organized Church. I challenge you not to tuck it away on your shelf after the first chapter, but to read it with an open heart. I pray Creator will use Sign Language to bring down the 'Feather Curtain.'

Mike Peters, Michigan
Ogimaw, 4 Fires Ministries

Terry Wildman has written a highly informative and well-balanced book addressing the injustices inflicted on the Native American people. In this book you will read stories, personal testimony, historical documents and Scriptures that shed light on the desperate need for hope, healing and restoration for the Native Americans. Anyone interested in gaining a better understanding of American history and God's prospective on revival and restoration for this great land should read this book.

Shannon Vinsonhaler, Florida
Author of *Divine Times*
Senior Pastor, Dove Assembly of God, Panama City

Terry Wildman has penned a prophetic historic overview of the plight of Native Indians in the United States. Extremely readable it underlines the immediate need for the church to pursue corporate repentance for the sins of our fathers upon these Native tribes and to pursue reconciliation and vindication of Native culture and society.

Ron Allen, Indiana
Lead Pastor, Heartland Church (www.heartlandfw.org)

ACKNOWLEDGMENTS

To my wife, Darlene, who has journeyed with me every step of the way as I discovered my Native heritage. Also for all the years of love and support as she has labored side by side with me in the ministry God called us to. And for her invaluable insights, suggestions, and editing that have found their way into this book.

To Casey Church, Bryan-Jon, and Michael Peters, my Annishinabe friends and mentors who have helped me to appreciate and love my Native heritage and the God-given beauty of our Native American cultures.

To Richard Twiss, who through his humor and hermeneutics, has helped me find a Biblical pathway to unite my faith in Jesus with my Native American heritage.

To the many Indigenous Nations and tribes of North America who have endured and persisted against the tide of injustice; and who have thwarted the attempted abortion of their inheritance and destiny.

To Gitchi Manidoo, the Great Mystery, who is God Most High, Creator of heaven and earth, redeemer of every tribe and tongue, and his Son Jesus Christ—my Savior.

Israel and the Gibeonites

Fourteen hundred years before the time of Jesus, Israel had just entered their promised land. Moses had died and Joshua was the newly appointed leader.

The people of Gibeon, who lived in the land, had heard about two great victories won by Israel. They worked out a scheme to trick Israel into making a treaty with them. The ruse worked and Joshua and the leaders of Israel swore an oath never to harm or attack the Gibeonites.

Four hundred years later, during the time David was king, a famine struck the land of Israel that had lasted for three years. King David prayed for direction. God revealed to him that Saul (King David's predecessor) and his family had attacked and killed many Gibeonites and were guilty of their blood.

David met with the Gibeonites in council and asked them how things could be made right again—so they could bless Israel. They replied that they had no recourse for restitution and no legal right to take revenge. David appealed to them again and asked what they wanted. The Gibeonites replied that since Saul and his sons had attacked and killed many of them, they wanted the death of seven of Saul's sons (Saul, at that time, was already dead).

King David responded, "I will give them to you."

The son's of Saul were delivered to the Gibeonites who then followed through with the agreement.

After that God answered the prayers for the land.

From Joshua 9:3–14 and 2 Samuel 21:1–14

Sign Language

A Look at the Historic and Prophetic Landscape of America

Terry M. Wildman

You know how to interpret the appearance of the sky but you cannot interpret the signs of the times.

—Jesus, Tribe of Judah

FOREWORD

In the early days of March, 1782, a group of Lenape Indians returned to their village on the banks of the Tuscarawas River to harvest crops from their abandoned fields and recover food they had stored for the winter. They were Christians, converted and nurtured through the ministry of Moravian missionaries David Zeisberger and John Heckewelder. The village they had established a few years earlier, which they had named Gnadenhütten (Cabins of Grace), was one of the first Christian settlements in the Ohio Country.

The village, however, was located in a war zone. Although the Revolutionary War was drawing to a close in the colonies, it continued unabated on the western frontier, where the British and colonists fought for possession of the Ohio Country through their Native American surrogates. The Lenape nation had been split by the conflict. One contingent chose to fight for the British. Another signed a treaty with the Continental Congress that promised the creation of an Indian state in Ohio, with Indian representation in Congress (a treaty never formally ratified in turn by the Americans). The Moravians constituted a third group that determined to follow a path of neutrality and peace.

In the autumn of 1781, however, the leader of the British-allied Lenapes ordered that the inhabitants of Gnadenhütten and its sister villages be removed north to a settlement on the Sandusky River. The Christians were not well-received by their Lenape kindred and received only meager rations of food. Within a few months they were starving. In February, they appealed to the tribal leaders and received permission to return to their villages to recover the food they had left in the fields and storage pits.

They were working in the fields when, on March 7, a detachment of Pennsylvania militia led by Colonel David Williamson arrived, bent on revenging the recent murders of white settlers. Upon seeing one of the villagers wearing a dress that had belonged to a murdered white woman, the colonists accused the Moravians of carrying out the attacks. Although the villagers responded that they had acquired the dress and other goods from a band of Shawnees a few days before, the militiamen would not let them present corroborating evidence. Instead, they rounded the entire village and confined the men and women in two separate cabins. They then deliberated what to do with them. In the evening a vote was taken. The decision was to execute everyone: men, women, and children. When informed of the decision, and of its finality, the Lenape Christians spent the rest of the night praying and singing hymns.

In the morning they were taken, two at a time, into the community meeting house, where their executioners bashed their heads in with wooden mallets and then scalped them. After all had been killed, the militiamen threw the ninety-six bodies into heaps in various buildings—twenty-eight men, twenty-nine women, and thirty-nine children, including infants—and burned the village to the ground. The charred remains of the corpses were later gathered up and interred together in a single mound.

When news of the massacre reached the colonists east of the Appalachians, there were scattered expressions of outrage. Yet no action was taken. Although some were appalled by the savagery of the deed, most chalked it off as one of the unfortunate atrocities that often happen in wars. No charges were filed, and none of the perpetrators was ever called to account by American authorities.

More than two hundred years later, in July of 2009, I visited the site of Gnadenhütten, along with Terry and Darlene Wildman and a small group of friends. The grounds of the village are now a historical park, flanked on the east and south by a cemetery. After walking through the modest visitors' center and strolling around the grounds, we gathered at the burial mound that now marks the southern edge of the park. We formed a circle around it. Terry played a hand drum and sang a song. We were quiet. We prayed. We were quiet again. It was hard to miss the small marker in the shape of an arrowhead that now stands at the north point of the mound. It reads, "Burial Site of Indian Martyrs," evoking a scene from the Revelation to John: "I saw beneath the altar the souls of those who had been slaughtered for the word of God and for the testimony they held. They shouted at the tops of their voices, 'How long, O Master? Will you not bring justice and avenge our blood on those who dwell on the earth?'" (Rev 6:9b-10).

Terry Wildman writes of a justice long-denied, not only for Native peoples who have suffered the loss of lands, livelihood, and life as the American empire spread across the continent, but also for those who struggle for life and liberty to this very day. Like the prophets of Israel, he seeks to correct our eyesight—to set before us God's vision and God's truth and to expose things that we, the American church, would rather not see about ourselves. Like the biblical prophets, he shoulders a burden that he bears out of love for God, the people of God, and the nation. Terry knows what God's ancient messengers knew, that right remembering is essential for right believing and right living. He not only sees the past well, he knows how to read the present and direct us into God's future.

This book will open up a new way of seeing. It will certainly disturb and unsettle you. If it does only these things, however, it will not succeed completely. In the end, this book should prod you to action. I encourage you to read Terry's words with an open mind and a responsive heart, recalling what God revealed long ago about what is good and what He requires of his people: to do justice, to love mercy, and to walk in a humble way with our God.

L. Daniel Hawk, Ohio
Professor of Old Testament and Hebrew
Ashland Theological Seminary
Author of *Joshua in 3-D:*
A Commentary on Biblical Conquest and Manifest Destiny

Author's Introduction

And the Pharisees and Sadducees came, and to test him they asked him to show them a sign from heaven. He answered them, "When it is evening, you say, 'It will be fair weather, for the sky is red.' And in the morning, 'It will be stormy today, for the sky is red and threatening.' You know how to interpret the appearance of the sky, but you cannot interpret the signs of the times..."

—Matthew 16:1-3

Learning God's Sign Language

Many people are concerned that something is wrong in America today. Most contemporary voices point to what has happened in the more recent past or even what is happening in our government and nation currently. I believe that it goes much deeper than that. The "tide of evil" some are warning us about today didn't just reach the shores of this land recently—it came here long ago. It was planted and incorporated into the founding of the United States of America.

There are many prophetic voices emerging in America today trying to interpret the *"signs of the times."* I am not implying that these prophetic voices are wrong, but I am proposing that we all need wisdom to interpret what we are seeing for *"We know in part and we prophecy in part..."* (1 Corinthians 13:9).

Today many are looking for answers, but so many of us are not asking the right questions. This book is more about searching out the right questions than in trying to present all the answers. I am aiming toward a landscape view—not trying to present all the details but more of a panorama.

Let's look at the present through the lens of the past and then from that perspective make an attempt to look to the future.

The intention of this book isn't to slam America. I grew up in this nation and have reaped its benefits—which are many. But this is not true for all who live here. Before you write me off as another America hater please read the rest of the story. There is much I respect and admire about America. I am not interested in bashing this country. I do, however, believe it is important that we have a realistic view.

My wife Darlene and I have spent the last ten years of our lives sharing Jesus with Native Americans. We lived among the Hopi Indians for five of those years, and have since visited tribal nations all across this land. We have seen with our own eyes the devastation that has been brought to this people group through the United States of America—and sadly through many church organizations who blindly and complacently cooperated with the government.

Because of the calling God has put on my life I began to embrace my own Native American Heritage. I am a mixed blood Indian and have Ojibwe and Yaqui ancestry. As I began to embrace this part of my heritage I discovered the pain and abandonment felt by the Indian peoples. This discovery has allowed me to view this nation and this nation's churches from a different perspective.

Professor and author James W. Loewen, who has extensively researched and written books on the subject of American history sees it this way:

There is a reciprocal relationship between justice in the present and honesty about the past. When the United States has achieved justice in the present regarding some past act, then Americans can face it and talk about it more openly, because we have made it right. It has become a success story. Conversely, when we find a topic that our textbooks hide or distort, probably that signifies a continuing injustice in the present. Telling the truth about the past can help us make it right from here on.[1]

How we view history really does matter. If our rearward vision presents a false horizon then our forward vision will also be skewed. If we don't accurately discern the past then our understanding of the present and future will be distorted. We will interpret the signs wrong!

Jesus wept over Jerusalem because its leaders and the people of his day both failed to understand *"the things that make for peace"* or recognize *"the time of [their] visitation."* Because of this they were not prepared for the judgment that was soon to come upon them. They interpreted the signs wrong!

And when he drew near and saw the city, he wept over it, saying, "Would that you, even you, had known on this day the things that make for peace! But now they are hidden from your eyes. For the days will come upon you, when your enemies will set up a barricade around you and surround you and hem you in on every side and tear you down to the ground, you and your children within you. And they will not leave one stone upon another in you, because you did not know the time of your visitation."

—Luke 19:41-44

---

[1] Loewen, James W. *Teaching What Really Happened: How to Avoid the Tyranny of Textbooks and get Students Excited About Doing History.* (New York: Teachers College Press, 2009),15.

I am often asked, "Why bring up the past?" But, the fact remains; every time we quote the Bible we are bringing up the past—whether good or bad. I believe the problems we face in America today find their roots in our beginnings. If we can dig down to those roots I believe we have a chance to see judgment averted—or at least lessened.

I am of the opinion that God's judgments are, for the most part, him letting us reap what we have sown—which means he doesn't intervene in that natural process. I believe that God has temporarily intervened many times in this nation to postpone judgment, but ultimately—if we don't get to the roots—time may run out.

If we don't, as the scriptures warn, judge ourselves, then we will certainly fall under the judgment of God (1 Corinthians 11:31-32).

Truth Justice and the American Way

Most of us who grew up in mainstream America were taught that it is *"One nation, under God ... with liberty and justice for all."* But growing up here has been a very different experience for the indigenous peoples of this land. Justice continues to remain illusive—like a carrot dangled in front of a horse.

The **"truth"** is that the **"American way"** has not been one of **"justice"** for the American Indian.

I believe it furthers the cause of injustice to cover up the sins of America. This nation could truly show its greatness by living up to its ideals, owning up to its failure to do so in the past, and then do what it can to make things right.

Many Native Americans experience a love/hate relationship with America as a nation. They love this land; it is the home of their ancestors. Many feel a deep unexplainable connection to the geographic and historic homeland of their tribe.

It might surprise some to know that by percentage of population more Indians serve in the Armed Forces than any other people group in America. I am an Army Veteran of the Vietnam era. At every powwow and most Native gatherings there will be an honoring of the American flag and of all the veterans who have served. American Indians are, for the most part, patriotic. However, many Natives are deeply disappointed in, and carry an undercurrent of anger and resentment toward the government. Why?

Imagine if you can, being born on an Indian reservation and learning at a young age that things used to be different— somehow better. What happened? A people came from another land and conquered our ancestors. They took away our way of life. Outlawed our ceremonies. Took the best of our land and forced us to relocate to unknown lands. They imposed their language and governmental structures on us long ago. Our children were removed from their homes and put into institutions for reprogramming. We were stripped of our language, our culture and our dignity.

We were told that all of this was done for our own good.

Today Natives are still fighting for their treaty rights, the rights promised to them in exchange for their lands. No treaty has been fully kept by the United States and many have been completely violated. Today's warriors are lawyers—they have to be. Just about every treaty right enjoyed today has been fought for and won in court, most of the time it took the Supreme Court to finally rule in their favor.

Is it any wonder that Columbus Day is seldom recognized or celebrated? How could it be? Many tribal governments stay open on this day as a silent protest to a forgotten past.

The Gospel (Good News) of Jesus and the Kingdom of God cannot be separated from issues of justice and righteousness. The very message of Jesus strikes at the heart of injustice. How can we as American Christians overlook the incredible injustices that have occurred in the past 400 years?

Yet today, many try to take the Gospel to Native Americans with the naive idea that a heaven vs. hell presentation represents the heart of the message. If we expect them to take this message seriously then we must address the historic and current issues of injustice that the Gospel of Jesus calls into question.

What can be done? What should be done? Most people are so caught up in their own problems, that to even consider the problems Indians face seems overwhelming. The issues seem to be too big to solve, better left to the Government.

But how does God see this? What is the commission of those who represent him?

> ...Learn to do good; seek justice, correct oppression; bring justice to the fatherless, plead the widow's cause.
>
> —Isaiah 1:17

> To crush underfoot all the prisoners of the earth, to deny a man justice in the presence of the Most High, to subvert a man in his lawsuit, the Lord does not approve.
>
> —Lamentations 3:34-36

If we want to see God's approval we can't afford to wait for the government to do it, and we shouldn't just blame our ancestors. Even though we can't change the past, we can impact the present and shape the future. Ultimately justice comes from God (Proverbs 29:26). It is the loving responsibility of those who represent him to be the ones who are seeking justice on behalf of those who are oppressed.

Overview

This book begins with **Foundations**, please take time to start there first. The rest of the book is divided into four overlapping parts.

Part 1 explores matters of God's justice as it relates to the founding of the United States of America and the dispossessing of the Native Americans. It includes a survey of the larger picture, going beyond American history to the roots of Colonialism and views Western Civilization in the light of Biblical prophecy.

Part 2 presents some possible and plausible historic and current "Signs of the times" for the reader's consideration.

Part 3 proposes a path of peacemaking that is congruent with the Gospel and offers practical examples of how we can cooperate with God and one another to see reconciliation and restoration.

Part 4 makes an attempt to glance into the future landscape of America; taking into consideration examples from Scripture and the historic and present signs of the times.

Listen to the Native voices of the past in the last part of this book titled, **Two or Three Witnesses**.

Throughout you will find quotations and footnotes. I would like to encourage each reader to go deeper; read the footnotes, check out the sources, and research these things for yourself.

I am convinced that one of the burdens of a prophet, after seeing God's perspective, is to call people into partnership with God to see that perspective become a reality.

I pray that the words of this book will stir us all to seek God for the humility to acknowledge our ignorance and for a clear interpretation of the *"signs of the times."* This will enable us to truly be Jesus' church in America and throughout the rest of the world.

FOUNDATIONS

I am an Indian; and while I have learned much from civilization, I have never lost my Indian sense of right and justice.

—Ohiyesa, Lakota

But seek first the Kingdom of God and his righteousness [and justice]...

—Jesus, Tribe of Judah

Righteousness and Justice

God's kingdom and his throne, which represents his rule and authority, have a foundation, something that it rests upon. Righteousness and justice!

> *Righteousness and justice are the foundation of your throne; steadfast love and faithfulness go before you.*
>
> *—Psalm 89:14*

In the New Testament the word "righteousness" combines the Old Testament concepts of justice and righteousness together into one word. So righteousness can be translated as justice and vice versa.

Jesus came from the Father to represent him on earth. As a human being he carried the Father's heart toward the oppressed and broken. As the perfect King he holds the scepter of God's justice and righteousness, which symbolizes God's authority.

> *But about the Son he says, 'Your throne, O God, is for ever and ever, the scepter of uprightness is the scepter of your*

24

kingdom. You have loved righteousness and hated wickedness; therefore God, your God, has anointed you with the oil of gladness beyond your companions.'

—Hebrews 1:8–9

God's judgment is coupled with his righteousness and justice. Judgment is not punishment but it is the setting of things right again, restoring them to God's original purpose. Judgment is corrective; to move those affected more toward his original agenda or to remove those in complete and stubborn opposition. Since the fall of Adam and Eve mankind has continued to fall short of God's glory. God's glory relates to the original purpose he has created all things for. When God restores the original purpose for anything in his creation, beginning with human beings, this is his justice or righteousness in action.

Restoring All Things

The final outcome of the Kingdom of God is the restoration of all things. Even though this will not be fully accomplished until Jesus returns, he is calling his followers to cooperate with him now to see restoration within the sphere of their influence.

That times of refreshing may come from the presence of the Lord, and that he may send the Christ appointed for you, Jesus, whom heaven must receive until the time for restoring all the things about which God spoke by the mouth of his holy prophets long ago.

—Acts 3:20-21

> *Then comes the end, when he delivers the kingdom to God the Father after destroying every rule and every authority and power. For he must reign until he has put all his enemies under his feet.*
>
> — *1 Corinthians 15:24-25*

Jesus has fully accomplished all that is needed through his life, death and resurrection, to bring his heavenly kingdom into the earthly realm. He is now working through the church, which is his council on earth, authorized, commissioned and empowered by his Spirit, to bring all things in this realm into submission to him.

In the following passage Peter, having received a heavenly revelation concerning the identity of Jesus, is representative of what God purposes for all his church.

> *And I tell you, you are Peter, and on this rock I will build my church, and the gates of hell shall not prevail against it. I will give you the keys of the kingdom of heaven, and whatever you bind on earth shall be bound in heaven, and whatever you loose on earth shall be loosed in heaven.*
>
> — *Matthew 16:18-19*

When believers in Jesus walk in this heavenly revelation they carry the authority of Jesus to bring all things under his feet and establish the justice or righteousness of God in the earthly realm. Until his return the church will continue to carry out the works of Jesus, setting free the oppressed, healing the sick, binding up the brokenhearted, announcing and demonstrating the reign of God, his kingdom.

A Scepter of Justice

In the ancient world of the Bible a King's scepter was the symbol of royal authority. The scepter of God's kingdom, according to Hebrews 1:8–9 is the loving of justice (righteousness) and the hating of injustice (wickedness or unrighteousness). God's throne is established on this foundation and is extended to others through his love and faithfulness.

Jesus' ministry, which was foretold by the prophets, is an extension of the righteousness, justice, love and faithfulness of God to Israel and then to the entire world. Matthew echoes the words of the prophet Isaiah and identifies Jesus' ministry as the fulfillment.

Behold, my servant whom I have chosen, my beloved with whom my soul is well pleased. I will put my Spirit upon him, and he will proclaim justice to the Gentiles. He will not quarrel or cry aloud, nor will anyone hear his voice in the streets; a bruised reed he will not break, and a smoldering wick he will not quench, until he brings justice to victory; and in his name the Gentiles will hope.

—Matthew 12:18-21

In this foundational prophecy Jesus is described as one who is empowered by God's Spirit in a radical and new way, showing the true purpose of justice from the perspective of God's kingdom. He is the victorious conqueror who makes sure that justice prevails! He speaks with humble dignity *"he will not quarrel or cry aloud,"* he brings an unprecedented gentleness, giving value and dignity to the oppressed and downtrodden *"a bruised reed he will not break, and a smoldering wick he will not quench."* This is the kind of ministry the nations are longing for!

Setting things Right Again

God comes to earth, in Jesus, to administer his justice—to set things right again.

> The Spirit of the Lord is upon me, because he has anointed me to proclaim good news to the poor. He has sent me to proclaim liberty to the captives and recovering of sight to the blind, to set at liberty those who are oppressed, to proclaim the year of the Lord's favor.
>
> —Luke 4:18-19

The "Year of the Lord's favor" refers to the Jubilee that God established for Israel. The following is adapted from Nelsons New Illustrated Bible Dictionary.

> The word Jubilee is related to the Hebrew word for a ram's horn, sounded on the Day of Atonement, and means to exalt or be jubilant.
>
> Debts were to be cancelled; those who had sold themselves into slavery, through debt were to be released. Since all land belonged to God it could not be bought or sold, but it could be lost because of indebtedness. In the Jubilee Year all land was returned to the families it had been assigned to by God.
>
> Part of the reason why God established the Jubilee Year was to prevent the Israelites from oppressing one another. This had a leveling effect on the culture; it gave everyone a chance to start over, economically and socially.
>
> The Jubilee reminds us that God wants people to be free. It stands as a witness to God's desire for justice on

Earth and calls into question any social practices that lead to permanent bondage and loss of economic opportunity.

One may also see God's provision for the land's conservation in the call for the land to rest. The people were not to extract the earth's resources in a greedy manner.[2]

The fruit of the Kingdom of God is *"righteousness [justice] and peace and joy in the Holy Spirit"* (Romans 14:17). This is what it is to produce. First God's kingdom produces justice, restoring things to their original purpose. Secondly it produces peace, this is the Hebrew concept of *the shalom of God* bringing wholeness, harmony, and security. Thirdly it produces joy, which it a heightened sense of well being, fulfillment and satisfaction. This joy relates to the *"oil of gladness"* and releases the anointing which is the presence of the Holy Spirit.

All of these are the results of God's kingdom and the sign of his reign. Those who represent God's kingdom will seek to bring justice, peace and joy to others within the sphere of their influence, through the power of the Holy Spirit.

Breaking Free of Dark Dominion

He has delivered us from the domain of darkness and transferred us to the kingdom of his beloved Son, in whom we have redemption, the forgiveness of sins.

—Colossians 1:13-14

---

[2] Youngblood, R. F., Bruce, F. F., Harrison, R. K., & Thomas Nelson Publishers. (1995). *Nelson's new illustrated Bible dictionary._Rev. ed. of: Nelson's illustrated Bible dictionary.; Includes index*. Nashville: T. Nelson.

We all must be rescued and become those who rescue others from the *"domain of darkness."* This dominion includes the dark worldly concepts and practices of power over others through worldly weapons and strategies. Through the Spirit of Jesus we are brought into a radically different kind of kingdom, one defined by loving; not just any love, but the kind of love the Father has for his Son.

Sadly, this is not how America or many of its churches approached the Native Peoples of North America. Instead of justice they experienced injustice, instead of peace they were forced into war, instead of joy they experienced sorrow and loss of all they knew. These are the fruits of oppression.

> *The Almighty is beyond our reach and exalted in power; in his justice and great righteousness, he does not oppress.*
> *—Job 37:23 NIV*

If the Kingdom of God is truly about seeking first God's righteousness and justice (Matthew 6:33), if it is about seeking restoration for the oppressed, about returning to God's original purposes; then what should our attitude be toward the original inhabitants of this land we call America? What would God's attitude be? In what ways can we cooperate with God's Spirit to see his original purposes for this land, and for the people he put here first, restored?

PART 1
AMERICA'S HISTORIC LANDSCAPE

History is written by the victors.

—Winston Churchill

To become different from what we are, we must have some
awareness of what we are.

—Eric Hoffer

America is false to the past, false to the present, and solemnly
binds herself to be false to the future.

—Frederick Douglass

History, despite its wrenching pain, cannot be unlived, but if faced
with courage, need not be lived again.

—Maya Angelou

CHAPTER 1

ECHOES OF LOST FOOTSTEPS

Lyrics by Terry M. Wildman

When you see a new trail, or a footprint you do not know, follow it to the point of knowing.
— *Uncheedah, Grandmother of Ohiyesa*

Walking on this road I'm wondering
What happened to the people of this land
Geronimo, Sitting Bull, Tecumseh
Echoes of lost footsteps in the sand
They are echoes of lost footsteps in the sand

Crying out for justice
Shaking like a leaf in the wind
Looking for the new day
Trembling in the palm of your hand
Yes, we're trembling in the palm of your hand

Walking down this road I'm asking
Will justice find a way in this land
Not that I require an answer
But I think I'll let the question stand
Yes I think I'll let the question stand

Crying out for mercy
Shaking like a leaf in the wind
Waiting for the dawning

Trembling in the palm of your hand
Yes we're trembling in the palm of your hand

Pausing on this road I'm pondering
Will a people who have faltered rise again
A Voice in the wind will answer
Echoes of lost footsteps in the sand
There are echoes of lost footsteps in the sand
Yes there's echoes of lost footsteps in the sand

CHAPTER 2

SEEDS OF A NATION'S GUILT

It makes my heart sick when I remember all the good words and broken promises.

— Chief Joseph, Nez Perce

Good Words but Broken Promises

The history of European contact with the tribes of North America is long, complex and intertwined with the wars between the Indians and Spain, France, Britain and finally the United States of America.

I want to give the reader a small glimpse into the beginnings of the history of America as it relates to the original peoples of America. We will overlook the first 200 to 300 years that the Spaniards, French and British were here, and focus on the United States of America shortly after it formed as a nation. This is not to say that those years weren't an important part of what happened, its just that those years go beyond the scope of this book.

Soon after the Revolutionary War was over the newly formed American Congress authorized the Northwest Ordinance of July 13, 1787. In it the US Government made the first promise to the American Indians.

The utmost good faith shall always be observed towards the Indians; their lands and property shall never be taken from them without their consent; and, in their property, rights, and liberty, they shall never be invaded or disturbed, unless in just and lawful wars authorized by Congress; but laws founded in justice and humanity, shall from time to time be made for preventing wrongs being done to them, and for preserving peace and friendship with them.

No sooner was this promise made than it was broken. Treaty negotiations were a slow process because the Indians were unwilling to give up their lands. Because the settlers couldn't wait they began to pour into the Ohio Valley region and soon there were bloody battles with the Indians. These battles became the excuse to attack the tribes and then began a pattern of forced and broken treaties that would last until all the land was taken except for the reservation lands—which became much like internment camps. In the taking of this land from the Indians not one of the treaties was kept in its entirety.

George Russell an enrolled member of the Saginaw Chippewa Tribe in Michigan tells the story of the treaties from the Indian's point of view in his book *American Indian Facts of Life.*

Typical treaty negotiations were based on huge Indian tribal land cessions in exchange for reservation areas, food, hardware goods and annuity payments. During the translation from document to reality, questionable sincerity succumbed to avarice and self-serving rationalization. The government's 'perpetual guaranty' of Indian tribal lands did not endure, and the delivery of food goods and monies failed to match the promises.

Indian tribes were at a distinct disadvantage during treaty negotiations because the treaty documents were written in a language Indian people did not understand. Treaties were interpreted to Indian tribal leaders who rarely knew what was actually written on the document placed before them for mark or signature. Other ruses included negotiation of a treaty with a manageable Indian who did not represent the tribe or plying the negotiators with whiskey.

Hundreds of treaties were negotiated between the Indian tribes and European settlers from early colonial days to the establishment of the United States. In 1778, the United States government entered into its first official treaty with the Delaware. At least 370 documented treaties were negotiated and ratified by Congress during the next 100 years.

In 1871, Congress declared that no Indian nation would be recognized for the purpose of making treaties. By then, Indian tribes realized that treaty negotiations had become a charade of empty promises based on fraud and deceit for the convenience of the government and the benefit of the land-hungry settlers.[3]

It became clear that it was greed, which the Bible calls idolatry (Colossians 3:5), that motivated the US Government and the people to behave this way. It seemed like the settlers and the government had a voracious and uncontrollable appetite for land.

Could the prophet Habakkuk's prophecy against the Chaldeans have an application for America?

Wealth is treacherous, and the arrogant are never at rest. They open their mouths as wide as the grave, and like death, they are never satisfied. In their greed they have gathered up many nations and swallowed many peoples. But soon their captives will taunt them. They will mock

---

[3] Russell, George. *American Indian Facts of Life*. (Phoenix: Native Data Network, 2004), 36, 37.

them, saying, 'What sorrow awaits you thieves! Now you will get what you deserve! You've become rich by extortion but how much longer can this go on?'

Suddenly, your debtors will take action. They will turn on you and take all you have, while you stand trembling and helpless. Because you have plundered many nations; now all the survivors will plunder you. You committed murder throughout the countryside and filled the towns with violence.

What sorrow awaits you who build big houses with money gained dishonestly! You believe your wealth will buy security putting your family's nest beyond the reach of danger. But by the murders you committed, you have shamed your name and forfeited your lives. The very stones in the walls cry out against you, and the beams in the ceilings echo the complaint.

— Habakkuk 2:6-11 NLT

Avoiding Responsibility

If we truly expected God to respond with justice to what America did to the Indians, would that cause us to humble ourselves and seek forgiveness? Or affect the way we see and pray for our nation? Would it motivate us to seek to reconcile with, and to help bring healing and restoration to our Native neighbors?

Many Christians become quite defensive when I bring up some of these questions. I get this response quite often, *"I didn't do this to them, it was someone else long ago, our ancestors who did this. Why would God hold this generation or anyone responsible for something they didn't do?"*

I don't believe that God holds individuals responsible for what their ancestors did. However, the Bible indicates that the

37

effects of the sins of our ancestors can be passed on (Exodus 20:5). Often the judgment of God is portrayed over entire nations in a corporate way, not just individuals (Isaiah 2:4).

As Jesus addresses his generation it seems that they hadn't learned anything from the past, they were essentially the same as their ancestors and he judges that they, under the same circumstances, would do the same things.

> Woe to you, scribes and Pharisees, hypocrites! For you build the tombs of the prophets and decorate the monuments of the righteous, saying, 'If we had lived in the days of our fathers, we would not have taken part with them in shedding the blood of the prophets.' Thus you witness against yourselves that you are sons of those who murdered the prophets. Fill up, then, the measure of your fathers. You serpents, you brood of vipers, how are you to escape being sentenced to hell? Therefore I send you prophets and wise men and scribes, some of whom you will kill and crucify, and some you will flog in your synagogues and persecute from town to town, so that on you may come all the righteous blood shed on earth, from the blood of innocent Abel to the blood of Zechariah the son of Barachiah, whom you murdered between the sanctuary and the altar. Truly, I say to you, all these things will come upon this generation.
>
> —Matthew 23:29-36

A close reading here suggests that Jesus considers that his generation was *"filling up"* the sins of their ancestors. As if the bowl was just about full enough to warrant an intervention— judgment. God judges, which means he implements his justice, he decides it is time for corrective action to restore his purposes. This is similar to God's word to Abraham about the sins of the Amorites not being complete (Genesis 15:16). This concept of the *"filling up of sins"* is also found in Revelation where it speaks of the *"bowls full of the wrath of God"* (Revelation 15:7).

Jesus discerns that the hearts of the scribes and Pharisees are so blind that they will do to his followers what their ancestors did to the prophets. Most Bible scholars agree that Jesus' prophecy was fulfilled (at least partially) in AD 70 when Titus surrounded Jerusalem with his armies, starved them out, slaughtered them and burned the Temple. Not all the people of Israel were in Jerusalem at the time, and Jesus even warned prophetically that those who saw this coming should flee (Luke 21:20-22). It is interesting to note that history recorded, through early church fathers Eusebius (325 AD) and Epiphanius (375 AD), that those who did heed His warning escaped.

Jesus also implies that this judgment had been brought upon them, likely a result of God letting them reap what had been sown. Perhaps confession and repentance would have brought about a different outcome.

Daniel Hawk, Professor of Old Testament and Hebrew at Ashland Theological Seminary in Ohio, gives some fresh insight into this subject from his book *Joshua in 3-D.*

> *How then might the accumulation of centuries of greed, theft, and seizure configure the American psyche? How might sinful patterns of conquest, consumption, and expansion exert an unrecognized influence of the way America thinks and acts? Why is there yet reluctance to expose and acknowledge the sins of the past, and to turn away from their effects on the present?*

39

A corporate perspective reveals that group sin does not fade away with time, any more than individual sin does. Without exposure, confession, and repentance, sin will work its way out in patterns of thought and action. A corporate perspective leads us away from a "past is past" attitude or a protest that says, "We weren't a part of that. That was someone else!" All who enjoy the fruit of life in the United States are the beneficiaries of practices and policies that sought to exclude, cleanse, and eliminate others. We should not labor under the delusion that we can be free of the effects of these acts unless we name the sins, repent of them, and do what is necessary to bring restoration.[4]

Ramona Big Eagle of the Tuscarora Nation located in North Carolina is a Legend-keeper for her tribe. Outside of that she is a motivational speaker and storyteller who speaks at Universities, Businesses, Schools, Camps, etc. When my wife and I stayed in her home in 2007 she told us an enlightening story of her experiences over the years when she has spoken at schools and camps for elementary age children.

She told us that she would often have a cup of water to drink during her presentation, in a Styrofoam cup, which would prevent onlookers from seeing what is inside. Sometime in the early 1990s on several occasions, after her talk, she noticed that some students would timidly ask her what she was drinking in her cup. At first she thought nothing of it, but as it continued to happen she began to ask the children what they thought was in the cup. The answer shocked her; they would reply "blood". When she asked

---

[4] Hawk, Daniel L. *Joshua in 3D, A Commentary on Biblical Conquest and Manifest Destiny.* (Eugene: Cascade Books, 2010), 99, 100.

them why they thought it was blood they would simply shrug their shoulders.

Ramona began to wonder why they would respond that way and sought God in prayer. It came to her mind that in movies and books Native Americans were often called "blood thirsty savages". She did some quick research and found this to be true. She then began to drink water at her presentations in a clear glass and found that the questions ceased. In 2002 she decided again to drink from an opaque cup, and yes, the question began to surface again.

This story is only one example of how deeply our national psyche continues to be influenced by the sins of the past, which still continues to be portrayed in our books and movies and in the unconscious attitudes of our children.

These deeply seated and often subconscious attitudes continue to work collectively among the people and leaders of this land affecting policies and influencing individual, corporate and governmental decisions.

A Fallen Perspective

America, as a nation, is guilty of many deep-seated sins and injustices relating to the original people of the land. Early on Indians were demonized and presented, in the writings of the period, as uncivilized and worthless.

Frank L. Baum, who would later write *The Wizard of Oz*, characterizes the mood of the public in 1891, just before the massacre at Wounded Knee; he writes this editorial published in the Aberdeen Saturday Pioneer.

With his fall the nobility of the Redskin is extinguished, and what few are left are a pack of whining curs who lick the hand that smites them. The Whites, by law of conquest, by justice of civilization, are masters of the American continent, and the best safety of the frontier settlements will be secured by the total annihilation of the few remaining Indians. Why not annihilation? Their glory has fled, their spirit broken, their manhood effaced; better that they die than live the miserable wretches that they are.

The early seeds of this kind of attitude can be found in the founding documents of America. In the United States Declaration of Independence, penned by Thomas Jefferson, this statement regarding the Indians is found in the grievances against the King of England.

*He has excited domestic insurrections amongst us, and has endeavored to bring on the inhabitants of our frontiers, **the merciless Indian Savages**, whose known rule of warfare is an undistinguished destruction of all ages, sexes and conditions. (Emphasis added)*

In the wars between the Indians and the United States savagery can be found on both sides. But it only takes a cursory reading of this history to determine who waged the most brutal and devastating forms of warfare. There are horrendous stories of brutal murder, mutilation and acts of genocide—by those who were calling themselves civilized!

David Stannard, Professor of American Studies at the University of Hawaii comments.

In 1783, Washington's anti-Indian sentiments were apparent in his comparisons of Indians with wolves: "Both being beast of prey, tho' they differ in shape," he said. George Washington's policies of extermination were realized in his troops behaviors following a defeat. Troops would skin the bodies of Iroquois "from the hips downward to make boot tops or leggings". Indians who survived the attacks later re-named the nation's first president as "Town Destroyer". Approximately 28 of 30 Seneca towns had been destroyed within a five year period.[5]

When these things are brought out into the open people sometimes say I am trying to play into what is called "white guilt". In our travels we often find white people with feelings of guilt about these things. However, I don't believe it does any good to try to produce guilt or assign blame to people today. This isn't about blame; it is about making things right again. I am also not saying that Indians haven't done their share of sinning. These were difficult times; of clashing cultures and worldviews that many believe could have not had a better outcome. Not that this excuses anyone; it is regrettably what happened. But the American churches could have, and should have, had a better witness and even now can work to see things rectified.

I want to remind the reader that one of the issues I am addressing in this book has to do with getting Christians to look at the history of this nation through the lens of Jesus and the Kingdom of God. If America, as many see it, started out as a Christian or even a Godly nation, it is difficult to account for the obvious and glaring sins perpetrated. Jesus said a tree would be known by its fruit (Luke 6:44).

---

[5] Stannard, David E. *American Holocaust*. (New York: Oxford University Press, 1992), 118-121.

Another View of History

America is a nation of this world and stands in relationship to God as intrinsically no different from any other nation. As believers in Jesus we are called to be good citizens of our nation and to always seek to live in peace and pray for those in authority (1 Timothy 2:1–2). In doing so, we need to be careful not to *"give to Caesar"* more than he is due—by making our nation out to be more than it is—which is a kingdom of this world.

When we try to make history conform to our beliefs, this distorts our view of what America is today, and what our role is, as members of the body of Christ, in relation to our nation.

For the most part the churches in America failed to be different enough from America to address the injustices that were taking place. There were a few voices of objection but they were neither frequent nor persistent enough to make the difference. Instead, many times the churches cooperated with the government by implementing governmental agendas such as the assimilation policies that gave birth to the church operated boarding schools designed to strip Native peoples of their language and way of life.

Many Christian groups hated the way the Indians were being treated and petitioned the government to let them be in charge of assimilation. But this only reveals a more serious question, what right does America, its churches, or anyone, have to assimilate Indians?

History records that church leaders and congregations sided and associated themselves with the government, and helped carry out the will of the government, which was to assimilate the Indians.

The history of Christian boarding schools stands as a testimony of how professing Christians had been assimilated to the ways of the world. Even some of the most pacifistic and untrusting of government churches such as the Quakers succumbed to this.

The greatest challenge of a Christian witness to the Indians today is how to answer the growing accusations of the Native Americans against the historic policies and practices of the churches.

As my wife and I travel this land to bring the message of Jesus to Native peoples, we hear the echoes of this history ringing in our ears, and find that much work needs to be done to first restore this brokenness, before the message will take root.

CHAPTER 3

KILL THE INDIAN
AND SAVE THE MAN

Carlisle Indian Industrial School, Carlisle Pennsylvania

The attempted transformation of the Indian by the white men and the chaos that has resulted are but the fruits of the white man's disobedience of a fundamental and spiritual law.
—Chief Luther Standing Bear, Oglala Sioux

There are many humorous things in the world; among them, the white man's notion that he is less savage than the other savages.
—Mark Twain

Solving the "Indian Problem"

Early in America's conflict with the Indians it became clear that the country lacked the manpower and resources to win a straightforward military victory. The strategy then became one of treaties, assimilation and removal. Leaders like Thomas Jefferson and William Henry Harrison planted the early seeds of America's assimilation and removal policies. This was their answer to the "Indian problem."

In a private letter, President Jefferson outlines America's assimilation policies, to the newly appointed Governor of the Indian Territories—William Henry Harrison. Harrison was granted broad powers over the territory that included present day Ohio, Indiana, Michigan, Illinois, Wisconsin and part of Minnesota.

President Thomas Jefferson to William Henry Harrison in 1803:

> *In this way our settlements will gradually circumscribe and approach the Indians, and they will in time either incorporate with us as citizens or the United States, or remove beyond the Mississippi. The former is certainly the termination of their history most happy for themselves; but, in the whole course of this, it is essential to cultivate their love. As to their fear, we presume that our strength and their weakness is now so visible that they must see we have only to shut our hand to crush them, and that all our liberalities to them proceed from motives of pure humanity only. Should any tribe be foolhardy enough to take up the hatchet at any time, the seizing the whole country of that tribe, and driving them across the Mississippi, as the only condition of peace, would be an example to others, and a furtherance of our final consolidation.*[6]

---

[6] Mintz, S. (2007). President Thomas Jefferson to William Henry Harrison, Governor of the Indiana Territory, 1803. *Digital History*. Retrieved 9/22/201 from:http://www.digitalhistory.uh.edu/learning_history/indian_removal/jefferson_to_harrison.cfm

One would think that if the Indians assimilated voluntarily they would have been accepted and done well. But the example of the Five Civilized Tribes in the Southeast reveals a different story. The Cherokee, as forerunners, quickly learned the ways of the Europeans, became educated by European standards and soon became very successful as plantation owners and businessmen.

The problem was these tribes were insistent on claiming their own lands and refused to "come under" the rules and laws of the states. They were their own nations, on their own land, and this became a sore point with the settlers, especially in Georgia. The Indians began to be more prosperous than the settlers! This eventually led to Andrew Jackson's infamous Indian Removal Act and the many Trails of Tears where these Civilized Tribes were all removed to Kansas, Oklahoma and beyond the Mississippi—and thousands died in the process.

Once the Indians had been defeated, moved beyond the Mississippi, and assigned to reservations, the government still intended to assimilate them—on its own terms. The US wanted them to relinquish all their rights as Indians and meld into life in the United States—lose their Indian identities. So hunters were forced to become farmers, they must learn to speak the proper language—English, they must build acceptable houses and dress properly.

Because the Indians were coerced into this arrangement they resisted assimilation efforts. The government and settlers had ruined the hunting grounds, killed off the buffalo, and placed the Indians into refugee camp conditions—poverty and hopelessness was rampant. America could not keep up with its promises to give training and tools—let alone feed all these people. This was the beginning of a *new* "Indian problem".

Carlisle Boarding School

A Civil War and Indian War commander Richard Henry Pratt in 1879 proposed a plan to the government that he believed would help solve the new "Indian problem"—and, in his mind, help the Indians.

To promote assimilation he suggested that Native American children be removed from their families and housed in boarding schools. In his opinion these schools would help Indians to claim their rightful place as American citizens. He believed that Indians should renounce their tribal ways, convert to Christianity, learn English and ultimately meld into the American way of life. This would be accomplished through discipline and education enforced in a military style.

Pratt founded, in 1879, the first of many of these boarding schools in Carlisle Pennsylvania known as the Carlisle Indian Industrial School. It became the template for dozens of these schools across America. Even though it was supposed to be voluntary many Native parents were coerced into giving up their children. Later children were taken even without permission.

The Indian children were housed barrack style, they were dressed in uniforms, their hair was cut, and they were assigned a "Christian" name. They were not permitted to speak their tribal languages—even to each other. Punishments for infractions became severe and there are many documented cases of abuse of the children physically and sexually. Because of overcrowding and poor nutrition diseases were common and many Native children died of smallpox, tuberculosis and malnutrition in these schools.

One hundred and ninety-two children are buried at Carlisle—most of them Apache. [7]

Over ten thousand Indian children passed through Carlisle Indian school, hundreds died and many more in the other schools that followed. Many failed to make the transition and returned home to their reservations.

Can you imagine what it must have been like for these young people to return home unable to communicate in their own language with their families? They were truly lost between worlds.

A Tree With Bad Fruit

Many boarding schools of this kind followed in other parts of the country, hundreds of thousands of Native children over the years have suffered in these schools. The psychological devastation on Native families from having children removed from their culture and entire family support systems has yet to be fully determined.

In 2010 my wife and I visited Haskell University in Lawrence Kansas, which was originally an Indian Boarding School established in 1887. There is a museum there that is dedicated to the memory of over 150 children who died at that school. It tells of many who were so traumatized by being removed from their families that they just wandered off into a nearby swamp—never to be found. A silent graveyard resides on campus that has stone markers to remember some of these children.

When I lived on the Hopi reservation I met a Hopi man who's Grandfather was sent to Alcatraz along with 18 other Hopi leaders who were resisting, peacefully, the assimilation policies.

---

[7] Landis, Barbara. *Carlisle Indian Industrial School History*. Retrieved from

The Hopis had become divided into what were called the "friendlies" and the "hostiles" in reference to their willingness to cooperate with the assimilation policies that included putting their children in boarding schools. When government bribes and coercion failed to produce results they sent soldiers to secure 104 children for the boarding school. The "hostiles" continued their passive resistance until this eventually led to the arrest of 19 leaders who were sent to Alcatraz! They spent nearly a year there before they were released.[8]

Church Involvement

Anyone who knows history, particularly the history of Europe, will, I think, recognize that the domination of education or of government by any one particular religious faith is never a happy arrangement for the people.

— *Eleanor Roosevelt*

A few philosophical and Christian groups were protesting the treatment of the Indians on the reservations. Even though these groups lobbied the government on behalf of the Indians— they still believed assimilation was necessary. As early as 1865 the government began to make contracts with various missionary societies to operate Indian schools.

The Quakers had approached the newly elected President Ulysses S. Grant with a proposal to give Christian groups and denominations charge of the affairs of the Indians. The Bureau of

---

website 9/23/2011. http://home.epix.net/~landis/histry.html
[8] See: Hopi Alcatraz Photos, Retrieved from website 9/23/2011, http://www.bethelks.edu/mla/holdings/scans/hopialcatraz/

Indian Affairs (BIA), which was full of corruption, was told to turn over many tribes to them. Soon denominations were assigned to Indian tribes by the BIA on the condition they would continue the policy of christianizing and civilizing them.

A Backward Step

Now it wasn't just the government oppressing the Indians but it was church organizations that were supposed to more directly represent God. This was a step backward from the perspective of the Gospel and the witness of the love of Jesus.

During the time I lived on the Hopi Reservation in northern Arizona I learned that when the Hopis heard the government was assigning Christian denominations over the tribes, they researched the denominations and asked for the Mennonites, since they were of pacifistic beliefs, and would use no weapons or fight in wars.

Unfortunately the church organizations did not fare much better. Harsh treatment and abuse continued in many places. If you speak with Natives today who remember boarding schools they will tell you their stories. Some had good experiences, but overwhelmingly the story is one of continued abuse from the clergy and Christian teachers and workers.

At one of our meetings in California an Apache man told me his "Christian" boarding school story, as he spoke to me he was fighting back tears. He said that the teachers would tie rubber bands to the front teeth of the Indian children and whenever they were caught speaking their language the teacher would snap the rubber band against their teeth.

Another Navajo man told me that when they cut his hair (which was a cultural shame) at his introduction to boarding school he and the other Navajo boys looked at paintings of a long haired Jesus and began to weep, not understanding why they had to have their hair cut.

A few years ago we were ministering at an Aglow International Meeting in Arizona where there were Natives and non-natives in attendance. As I spoke about these issues regarding the boarding schools and treatment of the Indians a Navajo woman came forward. She told us that God was convicting her of her need to forgive white people. Even though this woman was in Christian ministry she was still holding unforgiveness in her heart. With tears she told the story of her boarding school experience as a child. She said that the Native children were forbidden to speak their language and would be punished if they did. She was caught speaking in another language with one of her friends. Terrified she tried to explain that she wasn't speaking Navajo, but Spanish. She wasn't believed, and her punishment was to brush her teeth with Ajax cleanser! This didn't take place in the late 1800s—it happened in the 1960s!

There were many tears at that meeting as she told her story and repented to the white folks for her hatred and unforgiveness. Many responded to her with love and new understanding. One of the pastors in attendance told me that he wasn't "buying" my presentation until he heard her story—now he wanted to be involved with seeing more healing come.

White Man's God?

One tragic thing about these stories is that the gospel of Jesus gets associated with this kind of treatment. The gospel is supposed to be good news of the love of God through his Son but to the Indians who were in these boarding schools Jesus the savior began to look more like Jesus the oppressor.

Much confusion exists today among Indian people about the Gospel; many today call Jesus the white man's God. I don't believe that those who rejected this form of the Christian religion were rejecting Jesus; they were rejecting the false representation of him given by those who should have known better. Even today many churches and mission agencies on the reservations are still attempting to strip the Indians of their culture—thinking they are serving God by doing so.

American Assimilation

What can we learn from this? Hopefully we will begin to understand that the American culture has assimilated and infected our churches and Christian organizations. It has distorted our view of God's righteousness and justice. Historically American churches have been involved in partnering with a so called "Christian" government that has used the churches and believers to carry out its worldly agendas.

We need to be aware of this blindness and ask God to take the blinders off and help us to see how easily we can be deceived by the spirit of this world to cooperate with its dark agendas. We need to ask God for wisdom today as we are influenced by politicians and political parties that will try to win our votes and our numbers by using "Christian" slogans and manipulating us through our insecurities.

Many Christians pride themselves with being patriotic—but we must remember that our allegiance belongs solely to God—in Jesus. No earthly nation is worthy of the kind of allegiance and devotion we owe only to God. Yes, we need to pray for our nation. Yes, we need to be a voice of conscience. Yes, we should get involved in legitimate ways. But always with a healthy suspicion of government—especially when it is quoting scripture and co-opting Biblical language.

All governments, including America, represent differing forms of the kingdoms of this world that are under the control of darkness. Remember, one of Satan's schemes was to use the Scriptures in an attempt to manipulate Jesus. His strategies have not changed.

CHAPTER 4

NATIVE AMERICA TODAY

Overview

If you visit a public library or bookstore today looking for information about Native Americans, you will find about 95 percent of books end their history in the early 1900s. By this time the Indians had been removed to reservations and the western part of the US was being settled and developed. Once the Indian wars were over and they were assigned to the reservations they became, for the most part, out of the public site and mind—except as tragic romantic heroes. This produced a myriad of novels and booklets to feed a romantic and culturally curious readership.

Initially the federal government's relationship with the tribes was a combination of conquest, negotiation and treaty making on a government-to-government basis (1776–1828).

When they didn't go along with the US land hungry policies the tribes were then treated as sub-human with no rights; removal and relocation became their lot (1828–1887).

Once removed, relocated and assigned to reservations they endured land allotment and assimilation policies designed to rid them of their land holdings and tribal identities (1887–1928).

The US, in an attempt to relinquish treaty promises, implemented the Indian Termination policy and many tribes' federally recognized status and treaty rights were simply terminated (1945–1961). The termination policy soon proved to be a disaster and was repealed, but only after having a devastating effect on the tribes.

During the first half of the twentieth century the government experimented with the "Indian problem," implementing differing programs designed to alleviate the federal government's growing financial burdens.

In the mid twentieth century, after inflicting almost 200 years of untold damage upon the Indian Nations, the US finally began, unwillingly and under legal duress, to recognize and grant rights of self determination and governance to the tribes (1961—present).[9]

George Russell, in his book *American Indian Facts of Life*, comments on this historic impact with information from the 2000 US Census.

> *Third World conditions are still the reality for most of Native America and they are still the poorest race of people in the country in regard to health education and welfare. The prosperity of a handful of hugely successful gaming tribes has eclipsed the grinding poverty of the vast majority of American Indians.*
>
> *75% of the work force earn less than $7,000.00 per year. 45% live below the poverty level. The average unemployment rate is 45% and on some reservations is 90%. Most housing is inadequate and substandard. For instance, Navajos, who have the largest reservation and tribe with the most resources, endure the following conditions: 46% have no electricity. 54% have no indoor plumbing. 82% live without a telephone. These third*

---

[9] In 1983, Vine Deloria and Clifford M. Lytle in their book, *American Indians, American Justice,* outlined six periods of federal Indian policy characterized by the impact of federal actions for trying to resolve the "American Indian problem."

world conditions are typical of most reservation communities. Poor health care, miserable poverty and substandard education are a daily fact of life for most Indians.[10]

The historic devastation perpetrated upon the Indians is still with us today. The tribes that are federally recognized continue to experience the aftermath. But it is the tribes that have no federal recognition that have fallen through the cracks with little or no recourse.

Federal Recognition

Today many tribes are still unrecognized by the US Government. Some of these have obtained limited state and local recognition, while others are struggling to survive having no national, state or local recognition.

The following is adapted from website of the NCAI (National Congress of American Indians).[11]

Today many tribes are still seeking Federal recognition. There are roughly 562 federally recognized tribes in the United States, with a total membership of about 1.7 million. In addition, there are several hundred groups seeking recognition, a process that often takes decades to complete.

Federal recognition is important for tribes because it formally establishes a government to government

---

[10] Russell, George. *American Indian Facts of Life.* (Phoenix: Native Data Network, 2004), 41, 104
[11] Website retrieved 9/23/2011 http://www.ncai.org/Federal-Recognition.70.0.html

relationship. Through this recognition tribal governments can regulate their own people without state control. Funding and loans become available to provide programs for community services and healthcare.

The current process for federal recognition is a rigorous process requiring the petitioning tribe to satisfy seven mandatory criteria, including historical and continuous American Indian identity in a distinct community. Each of the criteria demands exceptional anthropological, historical, and genealogical research and presentation of evidence. The vast majority of petitioners do not meet these strict standards, and far more petitions have been denied than accepted. In fact, only about 8 percent of the total number of recognized tribes have been individually recognized since 1960.

At the present time it is the tribes who have no Federal recognition that are falling through the cracks. They have no help from the government, no casinos, no Indian health care, no treaty rights—such as hunting and fishing. Tragically, many tribes who are recognized look down on and offer little help to these struggling tribal groups. They are the outcasts of the outcasts! In a way they are orphaned nations, comparable to the widows and orphans that the Sacred Scriptures make a priority.

Indian Gaming

Contrary to popular belief, not all tribes have casinos. In fact, as of 2011, out of the 562 federally recognized tribes 240 have Casinos or Gaming on their tribal land. About one-third of these tribes distribute the money to individuals in the tribe.[12] Some of those only pay out a portion to tribal members and put the rest into community and business development. Sometimes the tribes buy back their own land with the casino money.

Regardless of personal opinions about gaming, our place as believers in Jesus is not to judge this practice, but rather to understand the benefits and pitfalls. Money doesn't usually solve problems and often creates them. I frequently hear criticism and judgment voiced toward Indians for Casinos, but seldom hear concerns or compassion expressed, or alternatives offered.

Indian's Today

Today there are reservation Indians, Urban Indians, Full-bloods and Mix-bloods, encompassing a wide variety of cultures and languages. Websites and periodicals such as Native Peoples Today[13] magazine and Indian Country Today[14] newspaper and network—all point to the durability and resiliency of America's First Nations Peoples. Native Americans are making movies, writing books and continue to influence the majority culture in unique and thoughtful ways.

Recently ABC's acclaimed 20/20 program did a first rate job presenting the struggles and the enduring spirit of the Lakota people living on the Pine Ridge reservation in South Dakota. The documentary is titled "Children of the Plains." The reader may still be able to view this on the 20/20 website[15].

---

[12] Retrieved from website 10/21/2011
http://www.nigc.gov/About_Us/Frequently_Asked_Questions.aspx#q_28
[13] http://www.nativepeoples.com/
[14] http://indiancountrytodaymedianetwork.com/
[15] Retrieved from website 10/21/2011
http://abc.go.com/watch/2020/SH559026/VD55148316/2020-1014-children-of-the-plains

This documentary gives a rare glimpse into the lives of Native Peoples today.

Native Americans are survivors; they may be the ones who will best endure the hardships that many living in the US may soon face.

CHAPTER 5

DEMYTHOLOGIZING AMERICA

It is my personal belief, after thirty-five years' experience of it, that there is no such thing as "Christian Civilization".

—Ohiyesa, Lakota

Do you call yourselves Christians? Does then the religion of Him whom you call your Savior inspire your spirit, and guide your practices? Surely not. It is recorded of him that a bruised reed he never broke. Cease then, to call yourselves Christians, lest you declare to the world your hypocrisy. Cease too, to call other nations savage, when you are tenfold more the children of cruelty than they.

—Joseph Brant (Thayendanegea), Mohawk

In a time of universal deceit—telling the truth is a revolutionary act.

—George Orwell

A Fearless Moral Inventory

One of the *"Twelve Steps of Recovery"* is to *"Make a searching and fearless moral inventory of ourselves"*.[16] I propose we do that very thing as we look at the history of America. The self-image of this nation contains the characteristics of a myth, especially in light of this nation's history with the Indians. According to today's dictionaries one meaning of myth is *"a popular belief or tradition that has grown up around something or*

---

[16] See: Website 6/23/2011 http://www.12step.org

someone; especially one embodying the ideals and institutions of a society or segment of society."

As we view the history of America it is hard to sort through the widespread hype and propaganda. Many have been so caught up in the popular image of America that they are willing to overlook the glaring inconsistencies. This seems to be especially true of those who consider themselves to be evangelical Christians. In a barrage of publications and websites, there is what appears to be a desperate desire to project a Christian image upon the founding of this nation. It is true that there were many Christian's who influenced its founding, but many of them were victims of their own cultural blindness.

When we hold any nation on earth, to the standard of the Kingdom of God, we find that they all fall short, and America is no exception. It is a common human trait to want to be proud of the nation we are born to. There is nothing wrong with finding the good in our nations, and America has done much good. However, we shouldn't think that the good it has done excuses its wrongdoings.

Many today are ignorant (which comes from the word ignore) of the true foundations of this nation. Even though the founding fathers used a lot of religious language with an emphasis on justice, they did not practice what they were preaching.

Few realize the irony that the US Capitol building was built by African slaves that were rented from their owners, and that an African slave named Philip Reid oversaw the casting and installation of the "Freedom Statue" on top of that building. It may come as a surprise that many of America's Founding Fathers were slave owners who became rich off the land stolen from Native Americans.

The American Way?

Many Christians in America equate "Truth, Justice and the American Way" with the Kingdom of God. Over the past few years, and especially during election season we have all been bombarded with email political propaganda—from Christians. The basic message is that America must return to its Christian foundation—as if there was a time that America was truly representing Christ, or that its foundation was Christian.

Gregory A. Boyd in the introduction of his book *Myth of a Christian Nation* cuts through the religious propaganda this way.

> *From the start, we have tended to believe that God's will was manifested in the conquest and founding of our country—and that it is still manifested in our actions around the globe. Throughout our history, most Americans have assumed our nation's causes and wars were righteous and just, and that "God is on our side". In our minds—as so often in our sanctuaries—the cross and the American flag stand side by side. Our allegiance to God tends to go hand in hand with our allegiance to country. Consequently, many Christians who take their faith seriously see themselves as the religious guardians of a Christian homeland. America, they believe, is a holy city "set on a hill," and the church's job is to keep it shining.*[17]

But when was America this shining light? Gregory A. Boyd continues to ask the right questions.

---

[17] *Myth of a Christian Nation.* (Grand Rapids: Zondervan. 2005), 12.

Were these God-glorifying years before, during, or after Europeans "discovered" America and carried out the doctrine of "manifest destiny"—the belief that God (or to some, nature) had destined white Christians to conquer the native inhabitants and steal their land? Were the God-glorifying years the ones in which whites massacred these natives by the millions, broke just about every covenant they ever made with them, and then forced survivors onto isolated reservations? Was the golden age before, during or after white Christians loaded five to six million Africans on cargo ships to bring them to their newfound country, enslaving the three million or so who actually survived the brutal trip? Was it during two centuries when Americans acquired remarkable wealth by the sweat and blood of their slaves? Was this the time when we were truly "one nation under God," the blessed time that so many evangelicals seem to want to take our nation back to?[18]

Again, I am not suggesting that all of American history is bad or unjust—America has done much good. It is a nation of good and evil, like other nations. The good that it has done does not excuse the bad any more than an admired business man, or politician, who has been discovered to be child molester, would be excused.

America is touted by many to be a nation that brings the light of freedom to the world. However this was not the experience of the original people of this land—instead they experienced the opposite. Their land and resources taken forcibly; they were imprisoned on reservations, denied religious

---

[18] ibid, 98.

expression, their families torn apart through relocation and boarding schools.

Ironically when other Nations used propaganda about America they didn't have to lie, they just needed to expose the "skeleton in the closet".

> *If we say we have fellowship with him while we walk in darkness, we lie and do not practice the truth.*
>
> *— 1 John 1:6*

Ideals are More than Words

> *I am tired of talk that comes to nothing. It makes my heart sick when I remember all the good words and all the broken promises. There has been too much talking by men who had no right to talk.*
>
> *— Chief Joseph, Nez Perce*

America has proclaimed some of the highest ideals of any nation on earth. There is much good in the ideals the founders proposed. But they were ideals not lived out, enjoyed mostly by those who were of the same ethnic group and persuasion as the founders.

Many Americans, especially those who are evangelical Christians, seem to have a selective view of the history of this nation. They tend to overlook or minimize the incredible injustices perpetrated against the Native Americans and many others in this land who are still suffering from the devastating effects.

> *Your eye is the lamp of your body. When your eye is healthy, your whole body is full of light, but when it is bad,*

66

your body is full of darkness. Therefore be careful lest the light in you be darkness.

—Luke 11:34-35

If we, as Christians in America, want to plainly see the Kingdom of God we need eyes—and hearts—that are clear, seeing things as they are, not as we wish they would have been. If our resources and prayers are spent on the wrong goals, or are based on a wrong premise, then we become poor stewards of the Kingdom of God.

I believe that much effort and energy is wasted trying to get America to return to its imaginary roots or attempting to use political power to get America to behave like a "Christian" nation. I don't believe it is the church's job to try to enforce Christian laws on the culture. Rather, it is to live out its beliefs as a witness to influence the culture by its actions. I believe this is what Jesus meant by exhorting his followers to be "salt" and "light" (Matthew 5:13–14).

My greatest concern is that the churches have married into the American dream and have been enamored by its propaganda. Furthermore, many Christian leaders and self appointed spokespersons continue to propagate this error until it is those who question it that become suspect.

The history of Christianity in this land has its dark side, a darkness worse than our government, since Christians should know better.

You can get a good outsiders view of the churches in America from the Native Americans, in the words of the Chiefs and Elders who saw through the hypocrisy. (See in this book: Afterword, Two or Three Witnesses).

Just a cursory look into the history of this Nation's relationship with the original peoples should awaken us and help us see more clearly the churches complicity in the demise of a people.

This complicity continues through the cultural haze that surrounds the churches today. We have found that church leaders in America are, too many times, completely unaware of the current condition of Native Americans. Even when it is made clear many still struggle to see any connection between what we have today and what we did in the past. It is hard to reconcile our beliefs about America and its "Christian" roots and what it did to the Native Americans.

Greg Boyd cautions us in his Christus Victor Ministries Blog dated August 16th 2010.[19]

> *Folks, it isn't anything more than an empty misguided claim that makes America a "Christian" nation. Until this destructive myth is dispelled and the true history of this country is brought to light, I'm afraid the American church will continue to look more like the racially divided, imperialistic, consumeristic, individualistic and hedonistic culture we live in than it will look like Jesus Christ.*

These are hard words to hear for many American Christians—but so were the words of Jesus to his generation and nation. Myths we are comfortable with are sometimes the most difficult concepts to dislodge from our minds and hearts. Maybe if we will view this nation through the experiences of the Indigenous peoples this will help us to dispel the myth.

---

[19] Boyd, Gregory A. *Lies My Teacher Told Me.* (7/14/2010). Retrieved 8/16/2011 from http://www.gregboyd.org/blog/lies-my-teacher-told-me

CHAPTER 6

AMERICA'S ANCESTOR WORSHIP

*The first missionaries, good men imbued with the narrowness of
their age, branded us as pagans and devil-worshipers, and
demanded of us that we abjure our false gods before bowing the
knee at their sacred altar.*

—Ohiyesa, Lakota

*You hypocrite, first take the log out of your own eye, and then
you will see clearly to take the speck out of your brother's eye.*

—Jesus, Tribe of Judah

The Judgment Measured Out

The churches of America have often judged Native Americans as guilty of ancestor worship. Many of our tribes have a belief that ancestors, relatives who have crossed over, are somehow able to watch over us, to guide us in some kind of mysterious, spiritual way. Also, there is a belief that these ancestors need to be honored and acknowledged in various ways. A common practice is to set out a plate of food for them at mealtime. There is concern that failure to honor these ancestors could cause them to be upset and unwilling to help. The particular beliefs and ceremonies involved differ from tribe to tribe.

Some churches have judged this practice as a kind of "consulting the dead" which is prohibited in the Bible. Many Natives I have spoken to see it more as an honoring of the ancestors, remembering that who they were still influences who we are today.

69

Some make a connection to the *"great cloud of witnesses"* spoken of in Hebrews 12:1.

This is one example of how American Christians judge and view Indian culture and their spiritual practices. Rather than try to understand and find ways to relate to it they arrogantly assume it is "pagan." They are blind to the fact that many of their own beliefs and practices could also be viewed in a similar way. Consider Easter egg painting and the associated Easter Bunny, which are "pagan" fertility rites, also prohibited in the Bible; practiced as part of the celebration of the resurrection of Jesus. This is only the tip of the iceberg! It is far too easy to be culturally blind and unable to see the *"log in our own eyes."*

Misrepresentation

The colonization of this land required that Native Americans be portrayed as savages, barbarians, and pagans so that the settlers would favor either their destruction or their removal. These attitudes continue to influence many today, especially in Christian churches, which are afraid of any spiritual practice or belief that is not experienced in their version of church. Many churches today reflect these attitudes in the suspicion and condemnation of anything Native.

We really have no right to be judgmental about these beliefs—especially to condemn people to hell because of them. Jesus did not send us to judge the world but to bring the good news about his love for all people and share the story of how he demonstrated that love.

> *For God did not send his Son into the world to condemn the world, but in order that the world might be saved through him.*   —John 3:17

Condemning attitudes toward the beliefs of others doesn't draw them to Jesus; many times it hinders them from hearing that message. My understanding is that all of us are already under the disapproval of God because we all miss the mark and fall short of his glory. It is through hearing the good news of God's love and the gift of his Son that we come to faith and are forgiven and delivered from judgment. Once we come to faith God gives us his Spirit to lead and guide us into all truth (John 16:13). We also have the Sacred Writings of what are called today the Old and New Testament to learn and be instructed from with the help of those gifted people he puts in our lives to help equip us.

Native Americans did not have the Bible to guide them about these things. The Missionaries from various churches took a harsh view of their beliefs about ancestors, judged them as pagans, and condemned Indians to hell for these practices. Many of these practices had been a part of their lives for many generations—threatening hell doesn't usually change deep-seated beliefs.

I am not saying that we can't question the beliefs of others. But we need to approach others with loving respect, not lording it over them but coming under them, with genuine love and humility. Patiently sharing our own faith and reasons we believe the way we do, using the Sacred Scriptures to illustrate our point.

A Confusing Witness

What hindered many Natives from hearing was the arrogance and hypocrisy they witnessed in the Euro-American brand of Christianity that was being offered them. This was evidenced in the differing beliefs and practices of the many church denominations, which were also condemning and fighting one another.

Another hindrance was the behavior of those who attended church. Natives were often taken advantage of and cheated, their land claimed and lived on without right. Many settlers incited attacks on them and then demonized them as uncivilized and savage when they defended their homelands and families.

The differing forms of Christianity and the manner that they worshiped God sometimes seemed outlandish to the Indians. They did not understand the church buildings with rows of hard wooden benches, with people sitting and staring at the backs of others heads, instead of in a circle; and one person did all the talking, the professional pastor/priest who insisted on being paid for his services. Traditionally a spiritual leader never charged for services in Native cultures.

In the eyes of the Indians some church practices seemed similar to their own. People prayed to saints who were dead and asked them for blessings and watchful care. Special gravestones and markers were placed at cemeteries to honor ancestors. These gravesites were treated like sacred places and visited by relatives of the deceased. Ceremonial flowers were placed at the sites and sometimes these Christians even spoke to their deceased as if the relative was present. All this was confusing and sometimes bewildering.

There is a modern story of an Indian and a white man visiting the gravesite of a relative. The white man noticed that the Indian had brought a plate of food and laid it on the gravesite. He rolled his eyes in ridicule and said to the Indian, "You don't really believe your dead relative can eat that food, do you?" The Indian looked at the gravesite of the man addressing him and replied, "Do you really believe your dead relative can smell those flowers?"

Apotheosis of George Washington

Many Christian Americans are unaware of this nations own form of ancestor worship. In Ancient Rome when a Caesar died they had a formal ceremony to elevate him to the status of a god— to be worshiped among the gods. This ceremony was called an Apotheosis, from the Greek meaning "the making of a god".

There is a painting, in the ceiling rotunda of our National Capitol building in Washington DC, that was commissioned by America's congress, and painted in 1865 by the artist Constantino Brumidi. It is called "The Apotheosis of George Washington".[20] The central image shows Washington surrounded by 13 female figures. The 13 figures are said to represent the original 13 states. To the left of Washington is the goddess Victory/Fame and on his right side is the goddess Liberty.

There are six other image scenes surrounding the central theme of Washington's apotheosis; going clockwise, they are the Greek gods "War," "Science," "Marine," "Commerce," "Mechanics" and "Agriculture."

The figures in each scene are gods and goddesses like Neptune, Mercury, Vulcan and Ceres and important historical figures of the time including Benjamin Franklin and Samuel F.B. Morse being taught by the goddess Minerva (Science) and Robert Morris (an important financial figure in the American Revolution) in "Commerce".

---

[20] See: Architect of the Capitol. *The Apotheosis of Washington.* Retrieved 8/16/2011 from http://www.aoc.gov/cc/art/rotunda/apotheosis/

Apotheosis of Washington, US Capital Rotunda
Photo by Darlene Wildman

America became enamored with the person of George Washington, elevating him to the position of a god. This attitude is still prevalent today and can be found in many government documents and educational systems. Take a look at what those who admire George Washington have prepared for High School age students of American History.

This is a portion of *The Apotheosis of George Washington*[21] written for high school students.

For more than 200 years, George Washington has represented the embodiment of "republican virtues" for America. During his lifetime, he was not only referred to as the "Father of his Country," he was even likened to the figure of Moses, leading his people to freedom. Beginning with his leadership in the Revolutionary War, Washington was loved and acclaimed wherever he appeared, whether it was en route to battle, on the battlefield, or at political appearances throughout the rest of his career. After his death in 1799, the high regard and reverence accorded Washington gave way to a full-fledged apotheosis, or deification, of this remarkable man. America began to immortalize its favorite hero and a plethora of paintings, sculptures, books, essays and speeches reflecting Washington's celestial personification began to appear.

The Log in Our Own Eye

Yes, many Americans have their own form of ancestor worship. Even Christians today have been highly influenced by this kind of propaganda. It is the *"log in our own eye".*

Rather than expose these ungodly attitudes and ideas many Christian organizations continue to reinforce the image of George Washington as a Christian to be admired. Even though he attended church there is much controversy today over whether or

---

[21] George Washington's Mount Vernon Estate & Gardens, Education Dept. Retrieved 8/25/2011 from
http://www.mountvernon.org/files/Apotheosis_of%20George%20Washington.pdf

not he truly identified himself as a Christian. Even if he did, then the depth and substance of his faith should be called into question. History is quite clear in the testimony that he was an active Freemason and held to the beliefs of Freemasonry. There is a website and monument building funded by the Freemasons in Washington DC dedicated to the memory of George Washington as a Freemason.[22]

Sometimes in an attempt to justify this some Christians have said, "People don't worship George Washington or bow before him and pray, so it's not really idolatry, is it?" However, idolatry takes many subtle forms and can be disguised. Worship isn't just bowing before a statue; sometimes it takes the form of bowing before an ideology. The word "worship" in Scripture can also mean "to serve," in this case is it possible that America idolized not just the person of George Washington but what he stood for? He became the icon of manifest destiny a sort of Moses or Joshua to lead the Americans to their destiny in this land. This mindset was embedded in the hearts and minds of the Euro-Americans who were, I believe, desperately needing a way to justify their consciences and adopt a religious facade for America.

If you still have doubt, consider also the statue of George Washington as the Greek god Zeus. It is a massive marble sculpture, reported to weigh as much as 30 tons, by Horatio Greenough who was commissioned by the US Congress for the centennial of Washington's birth in 1832. The statue depicts him as an Olympic God and is modeled after the ancient statue of Zeus, one of the Seven Wonders of the Ancient World. It was first placed in the rotunda of the Capitol until it cracked the floor and was moved to the east lawn of the Capitol building in 1843.

---

[22] See: *The George Washington Masonic Memorial.* Retrieved 8/17/2011 from http://gwmemorial.org

Because of controversy and criticism it was moved to the Smithsonian Castle and then finally to the National Museum of American History, where it currently resides.[23]

This sounds ridiculous to us today, but it reveals the condition of the "national psyche" in regard to America's founders. 2 Corinthians chapter 10 speaks of *"vain imaginations"* or *"lofty opinions"* that *"exalt themselves against the knowledge of God."* I believe that all who grow up in main stream America today have been infected by these vain imaginations and exalted ideas of our National identity. It is time for the church to put the axe to the root of the cherry tree and tell the truth about our past!

Even freedom can become an idol if we make that the ultimate goal, instead of serving God. Too many Christians equate democracy and capitalism with the Kingdom of God. The ideals of America are wonderful but many have allowed these ideals and good words to blind them to the reality of how America was really founded.

We find so many Bible verses quoted and carved into the walls of our nation's halls, but in reality they stand as a testimony against us. Christians in America love to point out how Godly our nation was at it's founding, but truthfully Christians were manipulated as our leaders quoted Scripture and wooed them with talk of righteousness, justice and equality. Could it be that America, as a nation, reflects the son in the parable of Jesus who says yes to his father but does the opposite?

> *Live as people who are free, not using your freedom as a cover-up for evil, but living as servants of God.*
>
> — *1 Peter 2:16*

---

[23] See: *The American Zeus.* Retrieved 08/17/2011
http://freemasonsfordummies.blogspot.com/2009/08/american-zeus.html

Those in America who consider themselves followers of Jesus and his humility should be the ones to see these things clearly. Lets open our eyes all the way and take an honest look at the tombstones that we have whitewashed.

It is time for the church in America to recommit itself to the holiness of the Kingdom of God. This will mean fully acknowledging our past and even current complicity with the sins of this nation. Then we can begin to move in a direction that is in alignment with God's purposes.

But before we can do this we have to separate the Kingdom of God and the church from national America in our hearts and minds. We need to understand that the darkness of the world has always been a part of America. That our christianizing of America has created a form of syncretism between the gospel and this nation. We have polluted the purity of the Gospel message by linking it to our national agendas, blending church and nation. This may be one of the main reasons so many Native Americans are unclear about the gospel and its message, and call Jesus "the white-man's God".

This form of "ancestor worship" that idolizes America and misrepresents the Gospel of Jesus needs to be turned away from. Perhaps the humility of repentance with the acknowledgment of the sins of the past and present could be part of the greatest witness the church in America could display in this generation.

The message preached is difficult for Indians, and other groups, to hear because it is laced with the history and actions of believers who represent a fallen nation more than they represent the Jesus of Scripture. When believers defend the injustices of the past or present, rather than expose them, the witness of Jesus in compromised.

As Darlene and I lived for over five years with the very traditional Hopi Indians we began to view the actions of the church from another perspective. This greatly humbled us and helped us realize how great the damage has been.

CHAPTER 7

WHITEWASHED TOMBS
AND MONUMENTS

*In the government you call civilized, the happiness of the people
is constantly sacrificed to the splendor of empire.*
—Joseph Brant, Mohawk

*Woe to you, scribes and Pharisees, hypocrites! For you build the
tombs of the prophets and decorate the monuments of the
righteous...*
—Jesus, Tribe of Judah

Jesus' words to his generation were hard for the nation of Israel to hear. Can we apply them to this nation and learn something? All across this land you will find monuments to the glory of men. You will see statues of the colonial leaders that are designed to inspire the imagination and warm the heart. There are even statues dedicated to the memory of the Native Americans who fought so bravely against them.

On the government buildings in Washington DC, you will find a mixture of Greek gods and Biblical characters. Huge obelisks, dedicated to persons and causes, silhouette the skyline. Scriptures from the Bible can be seen through out the city carved on the walls and monuments of the governmental structures. These Scriptures are often seen alongside the sayings of Greek philosophers. It is a strange and curious mixture. This is repeated time and again in most, if not all, of the State Capitols, and in many cities all across this land.

Rather than affirming the godliness of this nation they seem to stand as a testimony against it.

I would encourage every reader to visit your State Capitol, walk around and view the monuments, sculptures, murals and inscriptions. View them through the lens of God's kingdom and the teachings of Jesus and see what conclusions you draw.

Statue of Liberty

The Statue of Liberty is considered one of America's greatest monuments to freedom and opportunity. The following is a statement from the website of *The Statue of Liberty-Ellis Island Foundation*[24].

> *The Statue of Liberty is more than a monument. She is a beloved friend, a living symbol of freedom to millions around the world. These exhibits are a tribute to the people who created her, to those who built and paid for her, to the ideals she represents, and to the hopes she inspires.*

The statue was a gift from France to commemorate the 100th anniversary of the founding of the United States. It was finished in 1886 just over a decade late due to financial shortcomings.

Fort Wood, on Ellis Island, with its star shaped walls, a fort established during the war of 1812, often called "Tecumseh's War," was chosen as the base for the statue. The United States prepared the base and then France constructed and erected the statue on it.

---

[24] Retrieved 7/28/2011 http://www.statueofliberty.org/Statue_of_Liberty.html

The statue was modeled after the Colossus of Rhodes in ancient Greece that commemorated victory of the Rhodians against the Antagonids. The statue was erected to honor its patron god Helios and to express their gratitude for the military victory.

The Statue of Liberty faces eastward toward Europe holding high a torch representing the light of freedom. On a plaque attached to the base of the statue is the famous quote from the poem of Emma Lazarus, written at a fundraiser auction for the statue, titled—"The New Colossus".

Give me your tired, your poor, your huddled masses yearning to breathe free, the wretched refuse of your teeming shore. Send these, the homeless; tempest-tossed to me, I lift my lamp beside the golden door!

Even though this memorial has warmed hearts and inspired the admiration of several generations, it also represents a darker side to its history.

The United States needed more people from Europe to come and settle in the land. During the decade of the statue's construction the United States was pushing and expanding its boundaries westward into more of Indian territory. As the tribes resisted there was much blood shed; this was the period of "Red Cloud's War," "Custer's Last Stand," "Massacre at Wounded Knee Creek" and many other conflicts, as the tribes fought to protect their homelands.

As the United States removed the Indians they needed more settlers to help fight them and occupy the territories secured by war. Many from the east coast and Europe were lured west by reports from relatives and extensive advertising campaigns.

The ironic truth is, that as the US Government was beckoning Europeans to send their *"poor, wretched and homeless"* to America, it was creating *"poor, wretched and homeless"* conditions for its original inhabitants—the Indians.

INDIAN LAND FOR SALE

GET A HOME
OF
YOUR OWN
❈
EASY PAYMENTS

PERFECT TITLE
❈
POSSESSION
WITHIN
THIRTY DAYS

FINE LANDS IN THE WEST

IRRIGATED IRRIGABLE   **GRAZING**   **AGRICULTURAL DRY FARMING**

IN 1910 THE DEPARTMENT OF THE INTERIOR SOLD UNDER SEALED BIDS ALLOTTED INDIAN LAND AS FOLLOWS:

Location.	Acres.	Average Price per Acre.	Location.	Acres.	Average Price per Acre.
Colorado	5,211.21	$7.27	Oklahoma	34,664.00	$19.14
Idaho	17,013.00	24.85	Oregon	1,020.00	15.43
Kansas	1,684.50	33.45	South Dakota	120,445.00	16.53
Montana	11,034.00	9.86	Washington	4,879.00	41.37
Nebraska	5,641.00	36.65	Wisconsin	1,069.00	17.00
North Dakota	22,610.70	9.93	Wyoming	865.00	20.64

FOR THE YEAR 1911 IT IS ESTIMATED THAT 350,000 ACRES WILL BE OFFERED FOR SALE

For information as to the character of the land write for booklet, "INDIAN LANDS FOR SALE," to the Superintendent U. S. Indian School at any one of the following places:

CALIFORNIA: Hoopa.	MINNESOTA: Onigum.	NORTH DAKOTA: Fort Totten. Fort Yates.	OKLAHOMA—Con. Sac and Fox Agency. Shawnee. Wyandotte.	SOUTH DAKOTA: Cheyenne Agency. Crow Creek. Greenwood.	WASHINGTON: Fort Simcoe. Fort Spokane. Tekoa.
COLORADO: Ignacio.	MONTANA: Crow Agency.	OKLAHOMA: Anadarko.	OREGON:	Lower Brule.	Tulalip.
IDAHO: Lapwai.	NEBRASKA: Macy.	Cantonment. Colony.	Klamath Agency. Pendleton.	Pine Ridge. Rosebud.	WISCONSIN: Oneida.
KANSAS: Horton. Nadeau.	Santee. Winnebago.	Darlington. Muskogee. Pawnee.	Roseburg. Siletz.	Sisseton.	

WALTER L. FISHER,
Secretary of the Interior.

ROBERT G. VALENTINE,
Commissioner of Indian Affairs.

Mount Rushmore

This is an excerpt from the dedication speech of the Rushmore Memorial delivered August 10, 1927.

> *We have come here to dedicate a cornerstone that was laid by the hand of the Almighty. On this towering wall of Rushmore, in the heart of the Black Hills, is to be inscribed a memorial which will represent some of the outstanding features of four of our Presidents... The fundamental principles which they represented have been wrought into the very being of our Country.*
>
> *—President Calvin Coolidge*

For most of the Lakota and other Native Americans this monument stands as an ultimate insult to them. The Lakota people originally called Mt. Rushmore "The Six Grandfathers". This was in reference to their spiritual beliefs and sacred ways.

After the Plains tribes under Red Cloud had fought the United States to a standstill, the government signed the 1868 Treaty of Fort Laramie, which guaranteed that the Lakota would hold the Black Hills in perpetuity—that means forever!

This promise lasted six years and was broken after gold was discovered in the Black Hills. Slowly the land was whittled away by the US Government. In 1927, with this history as a backdrop, a white man living in Connecticut came to the Black Hills and dynamited and drilled the faces of four white men onto their Sacred Mountains. These were the faces of four of the Presidents who served in office during the confiscation of Indian lands and who shaped the policies of Indian removal.

How do Native Americans feel about this?

Here is the opening portion of a pamphlet that was handed out by The Lakota Student Alliance in 1996 in a peaceful protest at the Rushmore site. [25]

Mt. Rushmore is a desecration of our Sacred Mother Earth and a slap in the face of Lakota peoples everywhere. Documents have stated that Mt. Rushmore in the Black Hills of South Dakota is a shrine to democracy. As you read further, you will find that America was founded on the blood and lives of Indian peoples. We question what type of democracy this shrine represents.

The four faces carved on stolen Indian lands supposedly represent the four most notable presidents of the United States. With their ideals and values defined through the study of Iroquois society, America's founding fathers are indebted to the Lakota and all Indian peoples for their mere existence. But, in the Sacred Black Hills (our church, our synagogue, our temple) those presidents carved on that granite rock were more than mere democratic deviants.

The founding fathers on that rock shared common characteristics. All four valued white supremacy and promoted the extirpation of Indian society. The United States' founding fathers were staunchly anti-Indian advocates in that at one time or another, all four provided for genocide against Indian peoples of this hemisphere.

---

[25] See: *Mt. Rushmore is a Shrine of HYPOCRISY!* Retrieved 7/28/2011 from http://lastalli.blogspot.com/2010/08/lsa-history-mt-rushmore-gathering-1996.html

Mt. Rushmore is only one of many examples that could be given of America's monuments that have been whitewashed. Do monuments like this portray an image of America as being outwardly righteous but inwardly full of uncleanness and dead men's bones (Matthew 23:27–28)? How do you think Jesus would reply to this question?

Columns of Marrietta Ohio

In 2010 Darlene and I participated in an event sponsored by Glory International.[26] They believe that God has called them to ride horses across America to pray over the land and worship him as they ride. They often ride in places where there have been significant historic events, places that determined the future direction of this nation.

One such ride was in the city of Marietta, Ohio. Marietta was established on April 7, 1788, as the first permanent settlement of the Northwest Territory. This was the first colony established by the United States because the original thirteen were established by England. 1776 marked the beginning of the United States, and the birth of the first American Union Lodge of Free and Accepted Masons. This Lodge had no home until in 1790 where it found a resting place in Marietta Ohio. Settlers who were members of the lodge *"were anxious to erect an alter to Masonry in the wilderness"[27]*. George Washington's Masonic Apron was given to this lodge and displayed there for many years.

Marietta was the place where colonization started moving westward. In 1938 Congress authorized the erection of four pillar

---

[26] See: *The Glory! Ride*, from http://www.glory-international.org/whitehorses
[27] See: American Union Lodge No. 1 F. & A.M. *Part I, A Lodge is Born*.
Retrieved 9/23/2011 from
http://www.mariettamasonicbodies.com/au1history.htm

monuments one on each corner of the street along the park—
each bearing one of the following inscriptions.

*1st **Pillar:** Here the new United States of America
found, through Northwest territory, the first and common
offspring of thirteen discordant and disputatious states, her
formula to eminence among all the governments of
mankind.*

*2nd **Pillar:** To those unfamed citizens who conceived a
new purpose and direction for this nation in its making and
whose insistence upon incorporation of the "Rights of
Men" into our fundamental law set the pattern for
America's contribution to the governmental progress of
humanity.*

*3rd **Pillar:** Here with the founding of this Nation's first
colony and establishment of the first American civil
government west of the thirteen original states, began the
march of the United States of America across a continent
to the western sea.*

*4th **Pillar:** The Ordinance of 1787 contained the United
States first governmental recognition of the "Rights of
Men." Not included in the Constitution when adopted
they were later added until all of them are now a part of
our organic law.* [28]

Marietta, Ohio officially marks the place where the United
States decided to move westward and begin the process of
colonizing the entire American continent. It was the beginning of

---

[28] See: The Historical Marker Database. *Northwest Ordinance
Sesquicentennial Columns.* Retrieved 9/23/2011
http://www.hmdb.org/marker.asp?marker=20654

the end of a way of life for the American Indian, and a time of sorrow at the hands of a nation that is supposed to be founded on justice.

RainSong was asked to come and lead a time of worship and prayer at the park near the river, in preparation for the horses to ride the city. As we sang and prayed we looked with our own eyes at the whitewashed tombs and monuments that celebrate the founding of this nation.

As about 50 people gathered there to pray, we all asked God for forgiveness for what this place represents. For us that day, Ezekiel's prophecy to Israel had found its way to America. The foundation had been "laid bare".

> *I will tear down the wall you have covered with whitewash and will level it to the ground so that its foundation will be laid bare...*
> —*Ezekiel 13:14*

CHAPTER 8

ROOTS OF COLONIZATION

*Either make the tree good and its fruit good, or make the tree bad
and its fruit bad, for the tree is known by its fruit.*

—Matthew 12:33

A Transplanted Mindset

In the first part of this book a view of America has been presented that doesn't fit the popular ideas or image of this nation as a "Christian nation." Much of the confusion arises out of a mindset that was transplanted here from Europe. Spain, England and France were the primary nations who colonized America. These nations considered themselves to be "Christian" nations even though a similar glance at their histories would lead us to the conclusion that they were Christian in name only.

Colonization and Colonialism

These European nations practiced what is called colonization. Colonization is a process in which one country sends a group of settlers to another country to establish political control over its population and its natural resources. This is accomplished usually by force, through war, unless or until the people of the country come into agreement with its terms. They will usually only do this once they have been overpowered by the military might of the invading country or because they perceive the colonizing nation to be more powerful. This practice of colonization is so common that most people don't even consider colonialism to be a negative concept. In America we often hear the word "colonials" as a way to portray the founding fathers.

Colonial becomes an adjective to describe a certain kind of architecture relating to the early English settlers.

What are the roots of this practice, where did it originate? Why have people who consider themselves Christian practiced and endorsed these methods?

The Beginnings of World Empire

Colonialism in America finds its roots through Europe, and then further back to the Roman Empire. In the New Testament period Rome had conquered much of the known world. Rome considered itself the zenith of civilization and through its military skill and technology overpowered the indigenous peoples of their day and turned them into Romans. They would establish a colony to rule over the inhabitants and enforce upon them the Roman ways. Historians have coined this as "Pax Romana" or the "Peace of Rome."

The Book of Daniel, written 600 years before Christ, reveals there were to be four successive world empires. This was pictured in a dream, given to the King of Babylon. These empires were represented by a statue with a head of gold, chest and arms of silver, belly and thighs of bronze, legs of iron, and feet mixed with iron and clay (Dan. 2:32-33). Biblical historians agree that these depict Babylon, Medo/Persia, Greece and Rome. Rome was the fourth kingdom, represented by the legs of iron and the toes of iron and clay. This final kingdom was to be a divided one; broken into smaller kingdoms and would continue until the time when God would set up his kingdom that would replace them all (Daniel 2:44-45).

The Roman Empire was in decline when around AD 300 the Emperor Constantine converted to Christianity but continued his Roman ways under this guise. Constantine put the church leaders into power and the face of Christianity took on the spirit and character of Rome. Many Christian leaders were soon corrupted by their newfound status and the power they could wield. This militant style church, took up the sword of Rome, and began to extend its power by conquering lands and peoples throughout all of Europe. They would either assimilate and accept Christian baptism into the church or die.

Before its official fall around AD 400 Rome had already stamped its image upon the majority of those who represented Christianity. This form of Christianity influenced the nations of Europe, dividing into what could be represented by the ten toes of the statue.

This Roman based philosophy was eventually exported to the New World through the European nations that were trying to extend their influence and power. This was the birth of modern day colonialism. It is what western civilization and America is founded on.

The Coming Caesar

Consider this quote from respected Bible teacher Ray Stedman from his essay on *The Coming Caesar*.

> We have summarized here the strange course of Roman sovereignty over the earth. The fourth kingdom began with the Roman Empire, but, as the angel said to Daniel, it would be different from all other kingdoms. It is different because it is not a single nation dominating a great section of earth but it is a collection of nations. That is what marks the fourth kingdom as distinct. Remember that in Revelation 17 we were told also that the beast that appears there is made up of a multitude of nations and

tongues and kingdoms. It is a collection of nations and languages, dominating the world by the power of certain ideals and principles characteristic of it.

Now it is time to ask ourselves some rather revealing questions: Why is it that in the course of history since our Lord's day, all of the world's trade languages have been Western? Beginning with Latin (the language of Rome itself), which superseded Greek as the trade language of the world, we then have the rise of the Spanish empire when Spanish was the trade language. It was replaced by French up to modern times, but now it is English, which is spoken all over the world as the language of commerce, trade, and diplomacy.

Why is it that these universally spoken languages have always been Roman and Western? Why is it that Western dress has become the standard all over the world in our own day! Instead of the dress and cultures of the East, it has been the West that has conquered in this area. Western dress is now standard even throughout the Orient.

Why is it also that Western technology has spread everywhere throughout the world? **And why has the spread of Western civilization always resulted in the breaking up of indigenous cultures and has produced internal struggles among nations by industrializing them with all its inevitable accompaniment of congestion, pollution, and the ravaging of natural resources?** [Emphasis added]

Is it not at least possible that this is what is meant by the phrase, "It shall devour the whole earth, and trample it down, and break it to pieces"? Surely this is very *remarkable in the light of this strange prophecy. It seems quite clear that this fourth kingdom is indeed different from all the others that preceded it and has a strange and impressive effect upon the whole world.*[29]

Ancient Rome is not only reflected in much of the architecture of America's governmental buildings, but many historians observe that much of the internal structure of our government is also based on Roman and Greek ideals and philosophy.

This is not to say that other cultures have not had influence. Our Representative form of government was modeled after the Six Nations Iroquois Confederacy that Benjamin Franklin admired. The point I am making is that the Roman and Greek influence suggests that the feet and toes of the statue in Daniel's prophecy have extended into all the world, especially through nations that are considered to be "Western Civilization"—including America.

A First Hand View

Over the last few years Darlene and I have visited Washington DC twice as part of a prayer and worship event. As we walked the mall, visited the monuments, and stood at the front of this nation's capitol I heard, what I believe was God's voice, ask, *"What do you see?"*

I gazed at the giant marble columns and pillars, at the Greek statues of the gods and goddesses, the architecture of the rotunda, the frescos. The only answer I could reply with was "I see Rome". Everywhere we walked we saw the fingerprint of Ancient Rome.

---

[29] Ray Stedman, *The Coming Caesar,* (2/16/1969), Retrieved 9/23/2011 from http://www.raystedman.org/old-testament/daniel/the-coming-caesar. Used by Permission.

The Spirit of Antichrist

Colonialism and western civilization carries with it the spirit of Antichrist precisely because it misrepresents so much about Christ. Vines Dictionary declares that, *"Antichrist can mean either 'against Christ' or 'instead of Christ,' or perhaps, combining the two, 'one who, assuming the guise of Christ, opposes Christ[30]'"*.

John, an Apostle of Jesus wrote that the spirit of antichrist was already at work in the early days of the church.

> *Children, it is the last hour, and as you have heard that antichrist is coming, so now many antichrists have come.*
> *—1 John 2:18*

The spirit of antichrist carries with it a strong delusion (2 Thessalonians 2:11). How else can we explain the way that the church in America has so blindly participated in this holocaust of history? The name of Christ is usurped for its own purposes to carry out its world dominating agenda. It is the indigenous people of the world who have suffered the most under this spirit.

Perhaps it is the colonial powers that represent the iron in Daniel's prophecy—those with the might and power to dominate.

> *And there shall be a fourth kingdom, strong as iron, because iron breaks to pieces and shatters all things. And like iron that crushes, it shall break and crush all these.*
> *—Daniel 2:40*

---

[30] Vine, W. E., Unger, M. F., & White, W. (1996). Vine's Complete Expository Dictionary of Old and New Testament Words. Nashville, TN: T. Nelson.

It is the Indigenous peoples of the world that have been shattered and broken into pieces. Could they be represented in the clay that would not mix with the iron; that ultimately weakens the iron with their inability to completely conform? Indigenous peoples could be preserving agents weakening the advance of the spirit of antichrist.

> As you saw the iron mixed with soft clay, so they will mix with one another in marriage, but they will not hold together, just as iron does not mix with clay.
>
> —Daniel 2:43

This antichrist spirit rages against the Spirit of Christ and infects the nations with its poison (Psalm 2). It is the same spirit that deceived many through Hitler and tried to conquer the world and exterminate the Jewish people. It is the same spirit, working through colonialism that sought to exterminate and assimilate the Native Americans.

It can put on the fierce totalitarian face of fascism or even cloak itself in the friendly garments of democracy.

> And no wonder, for even Satan disguises himself as an angel of light. So it is no surprise if his servants, also, disguise themselves as servants of righteousness. Their end will correspond to their deeds.
>
> —2 Corinthians 11:14-15

The spirit of antichrist has been at work throughout the world seeking to displace the work of Christ, to create pseudo-kingdoms that would unite to stand against and even replace God's kingdom.

Like in Babylon of old, where mankind united in language and intention, worked against God's purposes, this spirit continues to this day trying to impose a single language and philosophy on the world. This is ultimately a futile attempt to return to the tower of Babel, where mankind was building an empire to *"make a name for themselves"* (Genesis 11:4).

The Nations Rage!

What can be done in the wake of such overwhelming, worldwide spiritual and human power? As the nation's rage against God's Messiah and his representatives (Psalm 2:1–3), what can we do to overcome this world and the spirit of antichrist?

> *For everyone who has been born of God overcomes the world. And this is the victory that has overcome the world—our faith. Who is it that overcomes the world except the one who believes that Jesus is the Son of God?*
> *—1 John 5:4-5*

By our faith in the Son of God we respond in an opposite spirit—overcoming evil with good. We follow Jesus' example by loving our enemies, blessing and doing good to those who would oppose us. Instead of judging and trying to control others we choose to love them and come under them to serve them. We pursue peace with everyone and work to see harmony and dignity restored between people. Through the love of God for his Son we labor to rescue those who have been oppressed and overcome by this dark world system. We live in quiet and unobtrusive ways always seeking the benefit of our communities. We pray for and honor the secular authorities so we can live in peace.

This is not some kind of passive neutrality, ignoring others and looking out just for ourselves; it is an active participation in doing the works of Jesus. We occupy the enemy's territory with the loving authority of the Son of God. In the spirit of his humility we bring comfort to the broken, sight to the blind, and healing to the hurting. Not a naive passivity, but an eyes wide open engagement of the enemy. We fulfill the words of Jesus who said, *"I am sending you out as sheep among wolves. So be as shrewd as snakes and harmless as doves."* (Matthew 10:16) NLT

Peter, one of the first followers of Jesus, sums it up here.

> *Be subject for the Lord's sake to every human institution, whether it be to the emperor as supreme, or to governors as sent by him to punish those who do evil and to praise those who do good. For this is the will of God, that **by doing good** you should put to silence the ignorance of foolish people. Live as people who are free, not using your freedom as a cover-up for evil, but living as servants of God. **Honor everyone. Love the brotherhood. Fear God. Honor the emperor.***
>
> *Servants, be subject to your masters with all respect, not only to the good and gentle but also to the unjust. For this is a gracious thing, when, mindful of God, one endures sorrows while suffering unjustly. For what credit is it if, when you sin and are beaten for it, you endure? But if when you do good and suffer for it you endure, this is a gracious thing in the sight of God. **For to this you have been called, because Christ also suffered for you, leaving you an example, so that you might follow in his steps.** He committed no sin, neither was deceit found in his*

*mouth. When he was reviled, **he did not revile** in return; when he suffered, **he did not threaten**, but continued entrusting himself to him who judges justly. (Emphasis added)*

— 1 Peter 2:13-23

The Apostle Paul echoes the same things.

*Bless those who persecute you; bless and do not curse them. Rejoice with those who rejoice, weep with those who weep. Live in harmony with one another. Do not be haughty, **but associate with the lowly**. Never be wise in your own sight. **Repay no one evil for evil**, but give thought to do what is honorable in the sight of all. If possible, so far as it depends on you, **live peaceably with all**. Beloved, **never avenge yourselves**, but leave it to the wrath of God, for it is written, "Vengeance is mine, I will repay, says the Lord." To the contrary, "if your enemy is hungry, feed him; if he is thirsty, give him something to drink; for by so doing you will heap burning coals on his head." **Do not be overcome by evil, but overcome evil with good.** (Emphasis added)*

— Romans 12:14-21

This is the beginning of understanding what peacemaking and reconciliation are all about.

PART 2

SIGNS OF THE TIMES

Whatever is has already been, and what will be has been before; and God will call the past to account.

—King Solomon, Tribe of Judah

Study the past, if you would divine the future.

—Confucius

It is said that the present is pregnant with the future.

—Voltaire

CHAPTER 9

NATIONAL HARVEST

The whites, too, shall pass—perhaps sooner than other tribes. Continue to contaminate your own bed, and you will one night suffocate in your own waste.
—*Chief Seattle, Suqwamish and Duwamish*

Just as the rich rule the poor, so the borrower is servant to the lender. Those who plant injustice will harvest disaster, and their reign of terror will come to an end.
—*Proverbs 22:7-8 NLT*

Reaping the Consequences of History

As I look at the problems America faces today I can't help but wonder how much is related to the seeds sown in history. If this nation as a whole has not named and turned from the sins sown at its founding, shouldn't we expect that these seeds would germinate through the generations to produce harvests, not of righteousness but of continued injustice? And wouldn't the churches of America, who for the most part, have identified this nation as "Christian" and participated in the sowing of those seeds, also be a part of reaping the consequences?

I have identified nine domestic fears and conditions that plague Americans today, including those associated with evangelical Christian concerns. These fears and problems represent only a small survey—it is not hard to identify many more.

I present these few for the reader's consideration, not as definitive declarations but more as observations to be reflected on, pondered and prayed about. I think the associations are surprisingly compelling and seem to correspond to many of the assumptions and warnings of the Prophets of old and Apostles of Jesus. In other words the Prophets, Jesus and the Apostles often used examples from the past as a link to understand the present. History does not happen in a vacuum and a pebble dropped in the past continues to reverberate into the future.

Fear of Terrorism

Terrorism ranks among the top concerns for Americans today. History records that another people, the Indians, also lived in fear of terrorism.

Let me tell you one of the stories from the early days of America's conflicts with the Indians. Prior to the American Revolution, a famous American leader, who at first admired the Indians, would later become bitter enemies with them. After the US had won its independence this leader ordered Revolutionary War commander, General Sullivan, to attack the Iroquois villages. His orders included the *"total destruction and devastation of their settlements"*. He ordered the crops to be ruined and as many hostages taken as possible regardless of sex or age. A military post was to be established in the *"center of the Indian Country"* with instructions to *"lay waste all the [Indian] settlements... that the country be not merely overrun but destroyed."* General Sullivan was told not to listen to any peace proposals until *"the total ruin of their settlements"* was accomplished. *"Our future security,"* he said, *"will be... in the terror... inspire[d]"* upon them.[31]

---

[31] John Sullivan to George Washington, 15 April 1779, in Otis G. Hammond (ed.), The Letters and Papers of Major General John Sullivan, Continental Army 3 vols. (Concord: New Hampshire Historical Society, 1939),3:1-5. http://www.earlyamerica.com/review/1998/sullivan.html

Who is the President that gave these orders to General Sullivan? Our first President—George Washington.

Yes, the "Founding Father" of America stated that the future security of America would rest on the terrorism it would inflict upon the Indians! Isn't it suspiciously ironic that today Americans fear for their own security against terrorists from other nations?

Another modern terrorist attack was anticipated through biological warfare. The British used smallpox as a weapon of biological warfare against the Indians. As I write this chapter today in Indian River Michigan, I am about 40 miles from the Lake Michigan coast where there once was an Indian village that extended from Cross Village to Seven Mile point—over 15 miles long! This entire area was ravaged when the British intentionally introduced smallpox to the Village.[32] There has been no documented proof that the US had an official policy of using smallpox, however history records that representatives of the government used it. This is a hotly debated issue and may not be able to be resolved until actual documents are found. In light of the documented atrocities that have already emerged, which include incidents of small pox as a weapon of war, it wouldn't surprise me if these documents eventually emerge.

Who can forget the anthrax attacks of September 2001 that threw the government and public into panic. While the first attacks were limited to a time period of only a few weeks, the widespread terror and alarm practically paralyzed the media and government.

Even though a modern smallpox attack never took place, there was still widespread government and public concern regarding its potential use as a bio-terror weapon. There was

---

[32] Blackbird, Andrew J. *History of the Ottawa and Chippewa Indians of Michigan*, Chapter 1, 1887, Project Gutenberg eBook, 2004

nearly a public panic over a shortage of vaccines available should such an attack occur.

September 11, 2011, marks the 10th anniversary of an extremist Muslim terrorist attack on what has come to be known as "Ground Zero" in New York City. A pastor of a church in Gainesville, Florida publicly threatened to burn the Muslim holy book, the Qur'an, on the anniversary of 9/11. This was likely in response to the announced building plans of a Mosque close to the Ground Zero site. Even though he changed his mind and promised not to, he later recanted. This pastor then announced he would hold International Judge the Koran Day on March 20, 2011, in which he staged a mock trial of the Qur'an, and burned the Muslim holy book.[33] I am glad to see many American Christian groups denouncing this act.

The aftermath of this has spurred a new wave of violence and retribution from radical Muslims, and a renewed barrage of hate statements and anti-Muslim propaganda filling the airwaves and the Internet—from Christians. There are still many who profess faith in Jesus joining and propagating this viscous rampage against Muslims, threatening with their own plans of Qur'an burning and worse. They may be standing upon the American rights of freedom of religion and speech, but tragically not on the teachings of Jesus.

At the beginning of the war with Iraq in 2003 the US Government quoted from the Bible to promote the war.[34]

---

[33] Timeline of Florida's Quaran-burning pastor (4/1/2011). Retrieved from CNN Belief Blog 9/23/2011from
http://religion.blogs.cnn.com/2011/04/01/timeline-of-floridas-quran-burning-pastor/
[34] See website retrieved 9/23/2011from
http://blogs.abcnews.com/thenote/2009/05/rumsfeld-gave-b.html

This practice, though encouraged by some Christians, makes the war seem like it is between Christians and Muslims—a holy war.

Regardless of our personal or national feelings about the building of this Mosque or even the Muslim terrorists, we as believers in Jesus should not respond with fear, hate and threats of violence—even in symbolic forms. Jesus taught us that we should love our enemies and do good to those who hate us. Are we following Jesus or are we going to be caught up in a nationalistic fervor that can only lead to more violence?

All of us grieve the loss of lives that occurred when the Twin Towers were attacked by militant Muslim terrorists. We should denounce all religious violence, in any of its forms, whether Christian or Muslim. We must resist the temptation to repay evil with evil. Just because we live in a land that says we can burn holy books to express our freedom of speech does not mean that we should. This is expressly true for those who claim to follow the way of Jesus.

The question must be asked, is this nation reaping, generations later, a harvest of religious based terrorism and intolerance, that was sown at its founding, in relationship with the Native Americans?

The Spirit of Abortion

Manifest destiny is the belief that God has given the Euro-American people the right to take ownership and rule over the inhabitants of the land and to claim it for the glory of God. This was influenced in the early assertions by the Puritans that they were the New Israel and America was the New Promised Land they were to inherit.

Their initial plan was to win over the Indians to Christ, but this proved to be a more difficult than they imagined. What do you do with those who won't convert? This line of reasoning led to the conclusion to drive them out of the land—and that is what they did.

I don't believe the spirit of abortion in America began with Roe vs Wade—it took root much earlier. Abortion is not just ending a life—it is the thwarting of a destiny. God has given a destiny to each person. Nations also have a God given inheritance (Deuteronomy 32:8), which ties in with the destiny of that nation. The Bible teaches us that it was God who *"fixed the borders of the peoples"* (Deuteronomy 32:8) and the *"boundaries of their dwelling place"* (Acts 17:26). When the Euro-Americans began to remove the Natives from their land and exterminate them as a people they were in essence aborting the destiny of the original inhabitants of this land, claiming it for a new destiny—a manifest destiny—that had no room for those who wanted to remain Indians.

This may be one of the reasons that all the efforts Christian and other right to life groups have made to stop abortion have not been successful. Could it be that we must first deal with a root of this sin of abortion that was perpetrated on the Indian Nations and individuals? Do we need to make steps to see healing and restoration come to them before we will see progress on this issue? It makes sense to me that God would want to *"lay the axe to the root"* (Matthew 3:10).

I find it quite ironic that currently in America there is one place where abortion is illegal—on an Indian Reservation. On September 17, 2008, the Tribal Council of the Turtle Mountain Band of Chippewa Indians enacted a resolution outlawing abortion on the tribe's reservation.

Here is the pertinent statement from the resolution.

> Be it further resolved that absolutely under no circumstances will abortions be performed and allowed within any private or public facility within the boundaries of the Turtle Mountain Indian Reservation and other lands under the jurisdiction of the tribe. The governing body faithfully believes that life is sacred and begins at the moment of conception between a man and a woman and life to be protected at all levels affirming natural law and reasoning... pro-life is a universal issue of common sense, moral righteousness for the common good of life.[35]

This decision by the tribe was influenced by their Traditional and Christian beliefs, which are predominately Catholic. It has caused quite a stir among members of the tribe and there are indications that it may not be able to be enforced. But since the tribe is federally recognized it can make its own laws. It has held to the date of the writing of this book, and perhaps it is a beginning seed of justice being sown into the land once again.

Those who were first set aside, who were themselves aborted as a people and a nation, are sowing new seeds.

Epidemic Greed

It seems that the last decade set new records for greed in America. This has been highlighted by the recent problems with

---

[35] Guedel, Greg. *Turtle Mountain Chippewa Enact Comprehensive Abortion Ban.* (Native Legal Update). *Retrieved 9/23/2011 from* http://www.nativelegalupdate.com/2008/11/articles/child-welfare/turtle-mountain-chippewa-enact-comprehensive-abortion-ban

the collapse of the housing markets that has devastated so many families. Government bailout of financial institutions, exposing the underlying avarice and uncontrolled greed that exists among its CEOs, has enraged millions of Americans.

Is there a connection between these out of control philosophies to the founding philosophies of this nation? To pay for its early wars congress had to promise land that was not theirs in payment for the service of soldiers. The eastern States under Andrew Jackson participated in the unconstitutional removal of the Cherokee, because the Cherokee held so much land—and the settlers wanted it! Over and over again it was America's expansionist policies, needing more and more resources, that drove the government to acquire the land from the Indians by any means possible—who cares if it is illegal or unethical.

America's belief in the policy of unlimited economic growth, which is unsustainable without more resources, found its origins with a voracious appetite for Indian land.

National Debt

America's early hunger for land and resources, along with its expansionist philosophy, was demonstrated in a private letter from President Jefferson to William Henry Harrison, the newly appointed Governor of the Indiana Territory.
Here is a small portion of that letter.

> *When they* [the Indians] *withdraw themselves to the culture of a small piece of land, they will perceive how useless to them are their extensive forests, and will be willing to pare them off from time to time in exchange for necessaries for their farms and families. To promote this*

disposition to exchange lands which they have to spare and we want for necessaries, which we have to spare and they want, we shall push our trading houses, and be glad to see the good and influential individuals among them run in debt, because we observe that when these debts get beyond what the individuals can pay, they become willing to lop them off by a cession of lands.[36]

Today America may be one of the largest debtor nations in the world, we owe a staggering amount, over 8 trillion dollars. Many analysts are concerned that our debt to China, America's number one foreign creditor, is so great that they could now be in a position to make war on us financially.[37]

The average persons debt ratio to income has skyrocketed in the last 50 years. Even though we are called the "richest nation on earth," the reality is we are living on borrowed money. This puts all of us in a precarious position. Consider what happened recently with the bank failures that required an embarrassing government bailout, that many believe only postpones the problem.

Could it be that our uncontrolled personal and national debt is one result of our earlier policy of driving Indians into debt with the intention of taking their land and resources?

[36] Mintz, S. (2007). President Thomas Jefferson to William Henry Harrison, Governor of the Indiana Territory, 1803. *Digital History*. Retrieved 7/22/2011 from
http://www.digitalhistory.uh.edu/learning_history/indian_removal/jefferson_to_harrison.cfm
[37] See: Herman, Arthur, *China's debt bomb* , New York Post *(2/8/2010) retrieved 9/23/2011 from*
http://www.nypost.com/p/news/opinion/opedcolumnists/china_debt_bomb_onc23nzJdiQR7gTLkrwSpL

Divorce and Family Breakdown

Could the high divorce rate in America today be somehow connected to the fact that this nation broke so many treaties, which are covenants, with the Indians? Marriage is a sacred covenant between men and women. The number of failed marriages that end up in divorce has grown to epidemic proportions. A report from the Barna Research Group reveals some startling statistics. [38]

The studies found that one-third of all married adults have been divorced at least once. Those who identified themselves as born again Christians had the same divorce rate! It appears that Christians and non-Christians share this problem in America equally. The national divorce rate (which compares the number of marriages to divorces each year) is over 50%, again those identified as born again believers fare no better, if not slightly worse.

Divorce is the ending of a relationship between a husband and wife, but this also affects the children—who have suffered the most. Families in America are being torn apart through the lack of respect for the covenant of marriage.

As a nation we tore apart Indian families through forced relocation and boarding schools—refusing to respect treaties, which are covenants. Children were removed from their homes and institutionalized, their cultural and tribal identities stripped from them. Today there is a crisis in American families. Lack of fatherhood, due in a large part to divorce, is creating an identity crisis among youth that leads to gang involvement in an effort to belong to something.

---

[38] See: *New Marriage and Divorce Statistics Released.* Retrieved 9/23/2011 from http://www.barna.org/barna-update/article/15-familykids/42-new-marriage-and-divorce-statistics-released

There is the unexplainable success of neo-Nazi groups and Islamic terrorist cells in their ability to recruit young and old Americans to their cause.

I believe all of this points back to the seeds sown in history.

National Obesity and Related Illnesses

You can't turn on your TV today without hearing about the health problems Americans face, that are related to the way we eat. Heart disease, diabetes and other illnesses are attributed to this problem. Many preach against drugs and cigarette smoking, and people die from those vices, but in the long run, even more lives will be lost to overeating and poor nutrition.

When Native Americans were removed to the reservations they were trapped there in internment camp conditions. They were not allowed to hunt, fish or gather foods in their traditional ways. This forced them into a situation where they were dependent upon the US government to feed them. They could no longer sustain themselves on the small portions of land they were relegated to. The land was often unfamiliar to them and not suitable for farming, which is what the government wanted them to do. The US government didn't keep up with the promised farm equipment and training. The treaties had guaranteed that the Indians would be provided with food until these policies could be implemented.

So they were sent food, called commodities, consisting primarily of sugar, white flower, lard, and cheese. For many generations the Indians diet had consisted of natural foods from the environment they lived in. The sugar, flour and lard wreaked havoc upon their bodies filling them with empty calories and poor nutrition. This diet resulted in obesity, diabetes and other related diseases. A sedentary lifestyle was the end result of being placed in these conditions.

Today obesity, diabetes and heart disease all run rampant in our society. The sedentary lifestyle of American children and adults is becoming the norm. Our healthcare costs are skyrocketing as a result of trying to cope with the health problems related to these issues. Grocery shelves are full of food containing starches, sugars, added salt, processed fats, coloring and preservatives. The recent demand for more nutritious foods has been responded to in the marketplace, but at higher costs, which the common person struggles to fit into their budget. The empty calories, fat and starches found in today's convenience foods are creating a generation of people who will suffer with a multitude of related illnesses. All this could lead to premature deaths and even further escalation of our healthcare costs.

Is it possible that what the US did to the Indians has come back to haunt us as a people?

Language Wars

There is a language war today in the USA between English and Spanish. Many Americans resent the fact that in some places Spanish is being accepted and used in schools and on marquees and traffic signs. It has become a divisive political issue as different States create laws to regulate languages. This issue probably won't go away in the near future as the Latino population continues to grow.

English isn't the original language of America, it is estimated that there were over 250 different languages spoken in the area the United States now occupies. Many of these languages are in danger of extinction and some have been completely lost.

The US government attempted to eradicate all the languages spoken by the tribes. This was enforced through the boarding school programs. Native students were not allowed to speak their language and were punished for doing so. English was enforced upon them as a means of removing their indigenous identities.

Here are some excerpts from the *Report to the President by the Indian Peace Commission dated January 7, 1868.*

> In the difference of language today lies two-thirds of our trouble... Schools should be established, which children should be required to attend; their barbarous dialects should be blotted out and the English language substituted... The object of greatest solicitude should be to break down the prejudices of tribe among the Indians; to blot out the boundary lines which divide them into distinct nations, and fuse them into one homogeneous mass. Uniformity of language will do this—nothing else will.[39]

The irony of this is the reality that during World War II, it was through Native American Code-talkers, primarily Navajos, that the US Armed Forces found an unbreakable code in the war against Japan. At Iwo Jima, Major Howard Connor, 5th Marine Division signal officer, declared, *"Were it not for the Navajos, the Marines would never have taken Iwo Jima."*[40] The very language the government was trying to eliminate may have been the greatest

---

[39] See: *REPORT TO THE PRESIDENT BY THE INDIAN PEACE COMMISSION, JANUARY 7, 1868.*Retrieved 9/23/2011 from http://history.furman.edu/~benson/docs/peace.htm

[40] See: Navy & Marine Corps WWII Commemorative Committee Report. *Navajo Code Talkers: World War II Fact Sheet.* Retrieved 9/23/2011 from http://www.history.navy.mil/faqs/faq61-2.htm

secret weapon of World War II and may have turned the tide for the Americans.

Religious Freedom

Perhaps the fears and controversy we experience in America today, in regard to religious freedom, finds its roots in our relationship to the Native Americans. Many Christian watchdog organizations are bombarding us with alarmist language about how if we are not vigilant we will soon lose our religious freedoms. A few of these claims may have some validity, however I am concerned that many Christians seem to only care about their own religious freedom while not showing the same concern for others.

It wasn't until 1978 that American Indians were granted religious freedom—yes, I said 1978! The previous denial of religious freedom to the Indians was highlighted in 1890 with the Ghost Dance. This began with a Paiute prophet known as Wovoka. He claimed a divine revelation from God that resulted in the practice of a peaceful nonviolent ceremony—that some called the Ghost Dance. The name came from the visions of the spirits or ghosts of ancestors and even of Jesus. Many different interpretations surround this dance, and it was seen by some as a similar belief that Christians held of the coming of a new heaven and earth.

On the Great Sioux Reservation in South Dakota many Lakota began to practice this dance.

This made the local Indian Agent nervous, so he requested government troops—which were dispatched to the location. The US Commander in charge ordered them to stop dancing, but in their own way they chose to obey the Creator rather than man, and suffered the consequences.

The Wounded Knee massacre was the result. One hundred fifty-three Lakota died that day, mostly women and children, murdered by the US Army using the weapon of mass destruction, for that time period—rapid fire light-artillery "Hotchkiss" guns. They were executed, massacred—why? Because they wouldn't stop dancing their prayers.

When Darlene and I visited this site we saw a historic marker calling it "The Wounded Knee Battle." Someone had crossed out the word "battle" and replaced it with "massacre." How could the use of automatic weapons against elders, women, children and babies be called a battle?

The Ghost Dance was outlawed. All across the nation Indians were forbidden to practice their spiritual ceremonies—which forced them to go underground.

There was no outcry by the Christian churches or groups that religious freedom was being denied. Was it because their own religious freedom was not being affected?

Today Indians are struggling with similar issues. Robert Soto, from McAllen Texas is a Lipan Apache Pastor who dances at powwows where he shares his faith in Jesus.

In 2006 he had his Eagle Feathers confiscated by a US Fish and Wildlife Service Agent who stopped a powwow and harassed vendors while searching for eagle feathers. [41]

Robert was bullied and threatened with arrest by this Agent who eventually forced him to surrender his eagle feathers. Because his tribe is only State recognized and not federally recognized, he cannot obtain the Federal permit to have an Eagle Feather. These feathers were passed down to him by his

---

[41] See website: Son Tree Native Path, *Feather Surrender Ceremony*. Retrieved 9/23/2011 from http://www.sontree.org/fs/Ala.htm

grandfather and are used to dance and pray with. Robert has been to court several times and has even won some small victories.

But the government is playing political games and wouldn't even show up at the last trial, fearing it might lose.

In the mean time Robert and a few other Native Americans are trying to get this law changed because it interferes with the practice of their freedom of religion.

I recently interviewed Robert Soto on the phone. Even though he has contacted Christian Magazines and Radio Programs the response has been only that of "We will pray for you." They have turned down his requests to be interviewed for a magazine article or a radio program. To date there has been no outcry from the Christian watchdog groups about this. For the most part none seem to care. Robert says he feels like a "lone warrior".

Why haven't the Christian radio stations and television shows or magazines interviewed him? Is it because the issue involves American Indians? Why is it the majority of American Christians are often unable to see beyond their limited cultural views, and care about the religious freedom of those outside of their box? Don't they realize that American freedom only equals "Christian freedom" when it includes other religions—whether Jewish, Muslim, Buddhist, etc.

God doesn't guarantee us religious freedom; quite the opposite Jesus predicted persecution, that the world will hate us as it hated him. But lets remember what he was hated for. It wasn't because he preached against the sins of society, but against the arrogance and hypocrisy of the religious leaders. Rome would have tolerated Jesus if it weren't for the religious leaders who accused him of treason before the Roman governor Pilate.

When Pilate asked them, *"Shall I crucify your King?"* they answered, *"We have no King but Caesar"* (John 19:15).

Many of them hated Rome but they hated, even more, the radical ideas Jesus was placing in the hearts of those who were following him.

Prayer in School

Getting prayer back in school has been a great concern among many Christian groups today. Many of the problems schools face today are cited as the result of prayer being removed from our public schools.

I am concerned that those who are pushing for this might be setting us all up for a greater problem. If prayer was to be restored to our classrooms what kind of prayer would it be? Who would do the praying? Who would we pray to? Would those who do not believe in God or prayer be required to participate? Will prayer be enforced on others?

This correlates to what happened to Native Americans. When children were removed from their homes and placed in government boarding schools, often church run, these children were required to pray to the "Christian God".

An Ojibwe woman elder, in Michigan, told a personal story to me in 2005. She said that during prayer, at the church run boarding school, the children were required to bow their heads when they prayed. As a young girl she was taught in her Ojibwe culture to always pray with your head lifted upward, so the Creator could see your face. To look down was considered disrespectful. This didn't matter to the Missionaries at the boarding school who punished them if they didn't bow their heads. Even though there are examples in the scriptures of bowing your head in prayer it isn't the only way to pray. It even says that Jesus *"lifted his eyes to heaven"* when he prayed (John 17:1). It is likely that the reason many Christians bow their heads when they pray is cultural and learned rather that from a deep sense of humility or in obedience to Scripture. There was no need to enforce this one style of prayer on these young Natives.

If public prayer is required again in public schools Christians might not be happy about who gets to do the praying. Christianity has long been the favored religion of America, but today the favor is shifting. Groups who represent other faiths are beginning to claim their rights also.

CHAPTER 10

SIGNS IN AMERICAN HISTORY

You know how to interpret the appearance of the sky, but you cannot interpret the signs of the times...

—Jesus, Tribe of Judah

If we will prayerfully and humbly look into the past and present, we may find that God has given some signs along the way to the people of the United States. Jesus said there would be *"signs of the times"* that we should heed. I would like to present just three interesting historic signs that may have been from God.

I don't present these as dogmatic conclusions but for the readers prayerful consideration. God often speaks in allegory and signs to give a message to those who are seeking him.

Give ear, O my people, to my teaching; incline your ears to the words of my mouth! I will open my mouth in a parable; I will utter dark sayings from of old, things that we have heard and known, that our fathers have told us. We will not hide them from their children, but tell to the coming generation the glorious deeds of the LORD, and his might, and the wonders that he has done.

—Psalm 78:1-4

Like the story in Daniel Chapter five of the handwriting on the wall that King Belshazzar of Babylon faced; God had numbered the days of his kingdom, he had been weighed in the balance, and his kingdom was given to the Medes and Persians.

Has God given this nation some similar signs?

Liberty Bell

The history of the Liberty Bell may stand as a historic and prophetic sign, revealing a flaw in the historic national identity of the United States. It was originally commissioned for casting by the Pennsylvania Assembly to commemorate the 50th anniversary of William Penn's 1701 Charter of Privileges. William Penn recognized and treated Native Americans as equals and established just policies and treaties with the Indians that lasted 70 years, until his sons broke the treaties.

A quote from Leviticus 25:10 *"Proclaim liberty throughout the land"* was inscribed on the bell. The bell cracked the first time it rang. It was recast twice and ultimately became unusable because the crack again became too severe. It is generally agreed that the final crack rendering it unusable happened on the celebration of George Washington's 100th birthday in 1846![42]

The Scripture in Leviticus inscribed on the Liberty Bell was to proclaim the Year of Jubilee, announcing the return of lost land and the setting free of those who were in servitude to pay off their debts. This is the Scripture Luke quotes as the foundation of the ministry of Jesus, who would *"set at liberty the captives and proclaim the favorable year of the LORD". (Luke 4:18-19)*

This stands as a testimony against America, not against her ideals, but against her practices. Africans were enslaved and the land was in the process of being unjustly taken from the Native Americans. William Penn's dream of justice and equality for the Indians was in shambles. It appears that God could not allow this bell to proclaim his liberty under false pretenses.

---

[42] *The Liberty Bell.* 05/10/2011 from http://www.ushistory.org/libertybell/

The Liberty Bell has become an icon of justice and freedom, but one that reveals a serious flaw. Abolitionists adopted the Bell as a symbol for the movement as a "cracked and fissured freedom for its black inhabitants." For Native Americans it stands as a huge question mark. When will our inheritance in this land be returned to us or at least recognized and honored?

The prophetic significance of this sign points to the need for the United States to acknowledge and rectify the wrongs done. God will hold this nation to the standard it has set for itself. Scripture teaches us that there is a greater responsibility upon those who are standard proclaimers. A greater judgment awaits those who take the role of light bearers or teachers.

Consider the words of Jesus and James in the New Testament.

> *The eye is the lamp of the body. So, if your eye is healthy, your whole body will be full of light, but if your eye is bad, your whole body will be full of darkness. If then the light in you is darkness, how great is the darkness!*
>
> —Matthew 6:22

> *Not many of you should become teachers, my brothers, for you know that we who teach will be judged with greater strictness.*
>
> —James 3:1

America often boasts of being the light of the world, but there is much darkness in America and in its history.

It's time for the churches in America to expose all the darkness, especially the darkness that disguises itself as a messenger of light.

Paul's letter to the Corinthians that warns against false apostles (messengers of Jesus), has an application to America.

> And no wonder, for even Satan disguises himself as an angel of light. So it is no surprise if his servants, also, disguise themselves as servants of righteousness. Their end will correspond to their deeds.
>
> —2 Corinthians 11:14

Believers in Jesus today must have a proper understanding of the times we live in and maintain a healthy skepticism toward our government's politics. The liberty promised by America has not been available to all people living in the land. If the churches of America fall out of favor with the government then they may experience the "crack" in our liberty and find themselves the objects of oppression. If we as believers put our hope in America for our liberty, instead of in God's grace, then we will, in the end, be greatly disappointed.

When the Earth Quakes

Earthquakes and natural disruptions in nature seem to be connected to the fall of Mankind. Adam was created from the earth and all of creation has been subjected to mankind's original disobedience. The Sacred Scriptures confirm that there is a great groaning and travailing of creation as it eagerly waits to be released from this bondage.

> For the creation waits with eager longing for the revealing of the sons of God. For the creation was subjected to futility, not willingly, but because of him who subjected it, in hope that the creation itself will be set free from its

121

bondage to corruption and obtain the freedom of the glory of the children of God. For we know that the whole creation has been groaning together in the pains of childbirth until now.

—Romans 8:19

This passage indicates that creation is subjected to mankind's sins and it somehow responds to the imbalance that man brings upon it—*"it groans in travail."* Native Americans have always believed that the natural world reflects the spiritual world. The Bible also indicates this in the following passage speaking of the Creator.

For his invisible attributes, namely, his eternal power and divine nature, have been clearly perceived, ever since the creation of the world, in the things that have been made.

—Romans 1:20

God's attributes are revealed through the created world, not only his goodness and kindness but also his wrath and anger. Creation is a living, active expression of God's divine nature and his ways.

Then the earth reeled and rocked; the foundations of the heavens trembled and quaked, because he was angry.

—2 Samuel 22:8

Consider also the following scriptures.

The earth lies defiled under its inhabitants; for they have transgressed the laws, violated the statutes, broken the

everlasting covenant. Therefore a curse devours the earth, and its inhabitants suffer for their guilt; therefore the inhabitants of the earth are scorched, and few men are left.
—Isaiah 24:5-6

The earth is utterly broken, the earth is split apart, the earth is violently shaken. The earth staggers like a drunken man; it sways like a hut; its transgression lies heavy upon it, and it falls, and will not rise again.
—Isaiah 24:19-20

It appears that God created the earth to respond to mankind's actions upon it. Adam's original act of rebellion effected all of creation, bringing a curse that causes its inhabitants to suffer for their guilt. There may be a cumulative effect that has been building since Adam's original transgression and then added to by the generations that follow (Romans 8:20–22).

As mankind continues to display, not the love and beauty of the Creator, but rather the rebellion and hatred of the Evil-one, *"The spirit that is now at work in the sons of disobedience"* (Ephesians 2:2), all of creation will continue to respond with violent birth pangs. The natural world affects the spiritual world and vice versa. The death of Jesus on the cross occurred in his physical body but his sacrifice affected not only the spiritual realm but also the natural. When Jesus died the earth responded! This was not a cumulative effect but an immediate response to what was happening in the natural and spiritual world. Consider this eyewitness report recorded by Matthew.

From the sixth hour there was darkness over all the land until the ninth hour... And Jesus cried out again with a

123

loud voice and yielded up his spirit. And behold, the
curtain of the temple was torn in two, from top to bottom.
And the earth shook, and the rocks were split.

— Matthew 27:25-51

The Roman soldier and other witnesses, that experienced the earthquake, took it as a sign from heaven.

When the centurion and those who were with him, keeping
watch over Jesus, saw the earthquake and what took
place, they were filled with awe and said, "Truly this was
the Son of God!"

— Matthew 27:54

It looks like the earth not only reacts to the cumulative effect of mankind's sins but in some cases when there is a very significant event it may respond more locally and in a closer proximity such as in the case of Jesus' death. These events can be signs to cause people to stop and consider what is happening, to seek God for further understanding.

When asked about the signs of his second coming Jesus responded with this answer.

There will be great earthquakes, and in various places
famines and pestilences. And there will be terrors and great
signs from heaven.

— Luke 21:11

I am not one who thinks that every tornado or natural disaster is some kind of direct judgment from God. Nor do I

124

believe that individuals or particular places affected by them necessarily reveal a particular censure from heaven. Jesus makes this clear to his disciples through the event of a tower that collapsed and killed several people.

> *Or those eighteen on whom the tower in Siloam fell and killed them: do you think that they were worse offenders than all the others who lived in Jerusalem? No, I tell you; but unless you repent, you will all likewise perish.*
>
> *—Luke 13:4-5*

Those immediately affected by the natural disasters aren't necessarily any worse "sinners" than those who were not. The locale may or may not be part of the sign. This leaves things somewhat open to interpretation and ambiguity but nonetheless God chooses to communicate some things in this way. When Jesus declared his purpose to a crowd God spoke from heaven and some in the crowd said it thundered while others said that an angel had spoken (John 12:29).

Regardless, we should still seek God for an understanding of the *"Signs of the times"*.

New Madrid

In light of this I believe we should consider the implications of the new Madrid Earthquakes.

The award winning historic novelist Allen Eckert recorded in his book *The Frontiersmen* that Tecumseh, in August of 1811, prophesied of a coming earthquake as a sign that the Indian tribes should unite against the encroaching United States. Many historians have a great respect Eckert, his novels are not fiction, and they are backed by great detail in historic research. Meticulous notes and references, including personal journals of many of the historic figures, document everything.

Tecumseh was a Shawnee warrior who's name means "Panther in the Sky" because the night he was born a great comet swept across the sky. Tecumseh was an Indian leader who attempted to unite the tribes against the encroaching United States and establish an Indian nation of combined tribes.

The most powerful series of earthquakes in the recorded history of Continental North America occurred in the winter of 1811-12. The epicenter of the final quake was New Madrid, Missouri on the Mississippi River.

The first hit on December 16, 1811, (2:15 a.m.) which was followed 6 hours later by another of equal intensity. Then January 23, 1812, (9:00 a.m.) another struck and finally on February 7, 1812, (4:45 a.m.) the final earthquake of the series hit. Modern research estimates the intensity to range from 7.0 to 8.0 magnitude. These quakes are referred to as *The Enigma of the New Madrid Earthquakes* by the *Center for Earthquake Research and Information (CERI)* at the *University of Memphis*.[43]

History documented that the Mississippi ran backwards. Lakes emptied and new lakes were formed. Water shot into the sky to the heights of the treetops. Fissures opened in the ground and belched out putrid sulfur across the countryside. Entire towns were destroyed. It was felt from Canada to the Gulf of Mexico. It rang church bells in Boston Massachusetts. It reached into Washington DC and woke the president in the White House. A

---

[43] Arch C. Johnston, Arch C. *THE ENIGMA OF THE NEW MADRID EARTHQUAKES OF 1811-1812*, (Center for Earthquake Research and Information (CERI), The University of Memphis, Memphis, Tennessee 38152, Eugene S. Schweig, United States Geological Survey and CERI, The University of Memphis, Memphis, Tennessee 38152)

million and a half square miles were affected. In between the quakes the earth was almost in constant motion with over 2000 aftershocks.

Tecumseh prophesied the coming of this quake as a sign from the Great Spirit for the tribes to unite. There was a great rallying of the tribes that resulted in the war of 1812 but many tribes failed to join and the battle was lost.

It is interesting and perhaps prophetic that the epicenter of the quakes was in the vicinity of the great Mississippi River. Up until that time the United States had only claimed the land east of the Mississippi. They were pushing the Indians beyond the Mississippi into what was then considered "Indian Territory" only recently acquired from Spain in the Louisiana Purchase.

The magnitude of these quakes, combined with what was occurring on the land, along with the prediction of Tecumseh should cause us to pause and ponder.

Is it possible that two centuries of war, greed, covenant breaking, land grabbing, and enslavement caused such spiritual turmoil that nature had to respond? Was this earthquake a message? Was God speaking through the earth? Was creation displaying God's displeasure with what was occurring on this land? Is it possible that God was saying, *"This far and no further— stop! Consider the consequences of your actions?"* As the Mississippi ran backwards were the purposes of God for this nation running backwards and having to find a new route?

The New Madrid quakes may have been a major *"birth pang"* as the earth cried out, *"Where are the sons of God! Where is the righteousness and justice of God they are to represent? When will it come?"*

Jay Feldman, whose writings have appeared in the Smithsonian magazine, in his book *When the Mississippi Ran Backwards* comments on this historic series of quakes.

> *The United States was at a turning point, one of those defining moments in history when forces converge so powerfully that something has to give. This was true geologically as well as historically—**it was almost as if the earthquakes were a symbol of the turmoil of the times.***
>
> *This is the story of the New Madrid earthquakes, but it is equally a story about America, and while it describes events that happened two hundred years ago, it is replete with themes and issues that reverberate down to the present day and continue to bedevil our nation: expansion, conquest, violence, corruption, greed, race relations, environmental degradation.[44] [Emphasis added]*

Was this earthquake also uncovering and exposing America's sins? A nephew of Thomas Jefferson, Lilburne Lewis, had in a drunken rage murdered, with an axe, an African slave in his household. This was in the presence of other slaves as a lesson for disobedience. He and his brother Isham then forced the other slaves to dismember him and burn up the body parts in the fireplace. The quake hit an hour later and collapsed the chimney, before the body was consumed, exposing this act of murder for all of America to see and remember.

In the same book, after telling the details of the above story, Jay Feldman reveals these insights.

---

[44] Feldman, Jay, *When the Mississippi Ran Backwards*. (New York: FREE PRESS A Division of Simon & Schuster, Inc.), 14.

The stories of Tecumseh and the Lewis brothers touch on two of the driving engines of early US History: Indian relations and slavery. Along with the country's shifting and dangerous relations with Britain and Spain, these two issues combined, on the Mississippi and Ohio Valleys' frontier, to create an exceedingly combustible era. The period between the end of the American Revolution and the War of 1812 has been generally overlooked, but in the West, those years were a perilous time that would determine the future direction of the nation." [45]

Each generation has opportunities to sow justice and righteousness, and to see a harvest of the same, or to sow seeds of continued injustice and unrighteousness for a dark harvest.

If our generation of Americans can read the signs, it seems we may be heading toward another set of birth pangs. Lets hope it's not too late to sow righteousness for a new harvest in America.

Sow for yourselves righteousness; reap steadfast love; break up your fallow ground, for it is the time to seek the LORD, that he may come and rain righteousness upon you. You have plowed iniquity; you have reaped injustice; you have eaten the fruit of lies.   —*Hosea 10:12-13*

Let's begin with the deepest root of injustice in this land—the Native Americans.

---

[45] (Ibid, 16)

2011 Virginia and East Coast Earthquake

While writing one of the final drafts of this book on August 23, 2011, an earthquake rocked Virginia and the east coast of America. Widespread damage was reported from central Virginia to southern Maryland including Washington DC. It was felt throughout the eastern US from Georgia to Maine and west to Detroit, Michigan and Chicago, Illinois and as far as southeastern Canada from Montreal to Windsor.

It is interesting to note that the quake was centered in Virginia the home of *Jamestown* the first permanent European colony. This is the historic place where the first treaties were made and broken with the Indians. It is also the place the first African slaves were brought to the colonies and traded.[46] It is the place where Native American and African American oppression began in this land.

If you look at a map of the original thirteen colonies you will find that this quake was right smack in the center and encompassed the region of all thirteen colonies.

Also to be noted, it cracked the Washington Monument in DC and crumbled plaster and paint from the iconic fresco of the Apotheosis of George Washington located at the dome of the rotunda.

The historic Washington National Cathedral sustained substantial damage in this quake. This cathedral represents the national place of worship attended by this nation's presidents and leaders.

---

[46] Lisa Rein, Lisa. Washington Post. 9/3/2006. *Mystery of Va.'s First Slaves Is Unlocked 400 Years Later* Website article retrieved 9/23/2011from http://www.washingtonpost.com/wp-dyn/content/article/2006/09/02/AR2006090201097.html

As of 2011 it has been 404 years since the founding of Jamestown, the place which the United States of America traces its beginnings. Historic sites, the thirteen original colonies, along with monuments and cathedrals are being shaken. Less than a week later hurricane Irene (meaning "peace") slammed the East Coast and Washington DC with brutal winds and flooding, leaving a wake of anything but peace.

> They have healed the wound of my people lightly, saying, 'Peace, peace,' when there is no peace.
>
> —Jeremiah 8:11

Is God drawing our attention to the roots of the founding of this nation?

Supreme Court

The Supreme Court is considered the epitome of justice for this nation and the world. The images carved into the facade of the Supreme Court Building include not only Moses but other famous law givers—men and gods.

Chief Justice Charles Evans Hughes during the ceremony for laying the cornerstone for the Supreme Court Building said, *"The Republic endures and this is the symbol of its faith."*

Perhaps we should follow this reasoning and consider the "symbolism" of the following event. On November 28, 2005, just before 10 a.m., a large piece of marble 10 by 12 inches broke away and fell from the Supreme Court Building's western facade. The chunk of marble broke away from above the words *"Equal Justice Under Law."* The piece of marble that fell was part of the molding that frames nine sculpted figures. The chunk that fell was over the image of Authority, near the peak and just to the right of the figure of Liberty, who has the scales of justice on her lap. The 172-pound chunk landed directly in the center of the path to the entrance and broke into about 40 pieces. No reason was ever officially announced but it has been speculated that it came from a flaw in the marble.[47]

If we follow this "symbolic sign" it could be a message that reveals a flaw in this nations practice of *"Equal Justice Under the Law"* and this is what weakens the *"Authority"* that *"Liberty"* is supposed to represent. Because of this the path to justice is being hindered for those who would try to enter.

I am sure some will consider this a stretch of the imagination but a quick search of the Internet regarding this event will show that I am not the only one who has speculated in this way.

Things that Make for Peace

I have presented these historic events as only a small sampling of many possible signs in history. I urge everyone to review the history of this nation in light of what was happening with the Native tribes and see if there is any correlation plausible.

Whether or not anyone agrees with my assessments is really not the point in this section of the book. They are simply to highlight the need that already exists to see reconciliation, restitution and restoration between the US and its churches with the Indians.

If they are signs from God, then they are to open our eyes, focus our attention, and spotlight the urgency of a swift response to those *"things that make for peace"* (Luke 19:41–42).

---

[47] 9/23/2011 from http://www.foxnews.com/story/0,2933,176881,00.html

PART 3
BLESSED ARE THE
PEACEMAKERS

Blessed are the peacemakers, for they will be called sons of God.

—Jesus, Tribe of Judah

If we have no peace, it is because we have forgotten that we belong to each other.

—Mother Teresa

If the white man wants to live in peace with the Indian, he can live in peace. There need be no trouble.

—Chief Joseph, Nez Perce

There is no path to peace—Peace is the path.

—Gandhi

If not us then who? If not now then when?

—Author Unknown

CHAPTER 11

CHIEF JOSEPH'S LAMENT

Lyrics by Terry M. Wildman
From the words of Chief Joseph

Then the Great Spirit Chief who rules above will smile upon this land and send rain to wash out the bloody spots made by brothers' hands upon the face of the earth. For this time the Indian race is waiting and praying. I hope no more groans of wounded men and women will ever go to the ear of the Great Spirit Chief above, and that all people may be one people.
— Hin-mah-too-yah-lat-kekht, Chief Joseph, Nez Perce

I will fight no more forever
We are tired we are old
Too many wounded sick and broken
Too many left out in the cold

Creator send your rain to wash the earth
To wash the blood from our hands
That we would be one people
That you would smile on the land
That you would smile on the land

On the trail of desperation
Driven from our fathers' graves
Empty words—broken promises
Will there be any left to save

My heart is heavy for my people
For I know that we must change
A way of life is gone forever
O Great Spirit feel our pain

CHAPTER 12

SINS OF OMISSION

I tell you the truth, whatever you did not do for one of the least of
these, you did not do for me.

—Jesus, Tribe of Judah

We are not punished for our sins, but by them.

—Elbert Hubbard

Reconsidering History

In Part 1 of this book we explored the foundations of
America from a different perspective, the perspective of those who
the Creator planted here first—the Native Americans. As we held
this nation up to the standard of God's righteousness and justice
we found, through this witness, that the United States falls far
short.

As we looked deeper we found that those who proclaimed
to be followers of Jesus, churches in America, were for the most
part complicit in helping to carry out the unjust national agendas
perpetrated on the Indians—in the name of God.

In Part 2 we looked at some possible historic signposts along
the way that may reveal God's warnings to America regarding the
treatment of those he placed here first. We explored the possibility
that nationally we are reaping the consequences of history—seeds
of injustice that have been passed on through the generations.
These seeds have produced, and continue to produce, harvests of
more injustice and imbalance.

Not Forgotten

Some might ask, what is your point? The past is the past. We can't change it. Why stir these things up? Someone might ask the Prophets and Jesus the same question. The simple reply is because it is important to God! He has not forgotten the original peoples of this land, and is not pleased with an attitude that would sweep it all under the carpet.

These things didn't happen that long ago, even from a human perspective. But from God's point of view, where a thousand years is a day and a day a thousand years, these things happened only hours ago. They are still fresh in his heart and mind.

The purpose of this historical journey has not been to assign blame or guilt but to bring understanding and insight into the history of this land so that we can see the present more clearly, and participate with God in those things that further his love and kingdom. We need to be able to identify what, if any, responsibility we have today for the sins of our American ancestors.

God Remembers

God remembered the covenant Israel made with the Gibeonites and held Israel accountable to it even though that covenant was approximately 400 years old. After he became King, David provided restitution to the Gibeonites, even though he did not break the covenant. His predecessor King Saul broke it.

The Gibeonites had tricked Israel into making this covenant to spare their lives, yet God still held Israel accountable to it. God even accepted the Gibeonites terms of the restitution, which was the death of Saul's sons, and removed the famine that was a result of the broken covenant (2 Samuel 21:1-14).

God also remembers the many covenants made by the US Government and the people of that government—many made in his Name. How can we even imagine that he would not hold this nation accountable for the hundreds of treaties, which are covenants, broken with the Indians?

Who is my Neighbor?

Even though no one living today may be personally guilty of the acts of injustice committed by our ancestors, are we guilty of not making it right again in the generations that followed? Jesus taught us that we were to be concerned about what is left undone!

> For I was hungry and you gave me no food, I was thirsty and you gave me no drink, I was a stranger and you did not welcome me, naked and you did not clothe me, sick and in prison and you did not visit me.' Then they also will answer, saying, 'Lord, when did we see you hungry or thirsty or a stranger or naked or sick or in prison, and did not minister to you?' Then he will answer them, saying, 'Truly, I say to you, as you did not do it to one of the least of these, you did not do it to me.
>
> —Matthew 25:42-45

The *Parable of the Good Samaritan* in Luke 10:25-37 illustrates this. I would like to present it in a somewhat "courtroom style."

An *"expert on the law"* wanting to "test" Jesus directs a question to him, *"Teacher, what must I do to inherit eternal life?"*

Jesus turns the question back on to the *"expert,"* *"What is written in the law, how do you read it?"*

The "expert" sites a safe written precedent, "Love the Lord your God... and love your neighbor as yourself."

Jesus offers advise, "Do this and you will live."

Wanting to justify himself the law "expert" replies with a misdirect to avoid accountability, "And who is my neighbor?"

Jesus testifies with a parable in response to his question. Here is a summary account of that parable.

> A traveler is robbed and beaten, stripped even of his clothes, and left for dead on the roadside. A Priest comes along and sees him but avoids the situation by passing him on the far side of the road. A Levite demonstrates the same avoidance. But then surprisingly, a despised Samaritan comes along and takes pity on the man. He does what he can to patch his wounds and spends his own money to put him up and have him cared for.

After sharing this parable, Jesus redirects with a question, "Which of these three do you think was a neighbor to the man who fell into the hands of robbers?"

The "expert" relinquishes and admits, "The one who had mercy on him." Jesus rests his case, and declares, "Go and do likewise."

I have found this lawyer's attitude to be prevalent today as I present a case for the Native Americans. Those who love their neighbor won't leave them destitute; love takes the form of caring and compassionate responsibility toward others.

The "sins of omission" are about not doing what should be done. In relationship to the Indians it appears that this kind of sin is the primary concern for the church in America today. Those of us who are a part of the American church continue to live off the benefits of broken treaties and the resources of stolen land, happy to reap the benefits, but denying any responsibility. All the while Native Americans are still, *"Stripped and battered,"* reeling from the historic impact.

It's time to love our Native American neighbors as ourselves!

A Lesson for Today

In light of the history of America and its churches, combined with the ongoing sins of omission, what lessons can we learn from the Scriptures? Do they continue to speak to us today? Can we apply them to the questions raised in this book?

The New Testament teaches us that the things that happened to Israel were to serve as an example for us today (1 Corinthians 10:11). Not only that, but it also shows how God dealt with other nations in the past such as Sodom and Gomorrah as an example (Jude 7). You might think, from this verse, it was primarily for their sexual sins that they were judged. Many Christians today think this is one of the primary reasons God will judge America. Even though sexual perversion is a sin it seems that other sins rank higher as a concern to God. A further look into the sins of Sodom reveals a different perspective.

> *Now this was the sin of your sister Sodom: She and her daughters were arrogant, overfed and unconcerned; they did not help the poor and needy. They were haughty and did detestable things before me. Therefore I did away with them as you have seen.*
>
> *—Ezekiel 16:49-50 NIV*

It seems evident that God judged Sodom for its attitudes of superiority manifested in presumptuous claims and assumptions (haughty and arrogant); but also because they were overfed and unconcerned about the needs of others, especially the poor and oppressed, and because they did detestable things.

Based on these criteria we should all be humbled at the patience and forbearance of God over the sins of this nation in relationship to the Native peoples.

Is it time for God to bring closure? Is this the generation?

Diane Wigstone, a descendant of Pocahontas, proposes this in her book, *14 Generations, America's Critical Choice for Blessing or Exile*[48]. She tells of how God revealed to her that it has been fourteen generations since the founding of Jamestown, America's first permanent European settlement. He showed her how he does things in cycles of fourteen generations (Matthew 1:17). She checked her own generation back to Pocahontas and found that she is the fourteenth.

In 2007 America celebrated its 400-year anniversary of the founding of Jamestown[49]; the same period of time Israel was enslaved by Egypt.

Perhaps this is the generation of Americans that God will call to account. If so I hope he finds his church in America working hard for reconciliation, healing and restoration among its original inhabitants.

---

[48] See: Wigstone, Diane. *14 Generations, Americas Critical Choice for Blessing or Exile.* (Arlington: Kingdom Enterprises International Publishing, 2005)

[49] See website: *America's 400th Anniversary Legacy.* Retrieved http://www.jamestown2007.org/

A Faltering Apology

Hasn't the United States apologized to the Native Americans? The answer to that is, yes—and no. Even though Australia and Canada have both publicly apologized in 2008 for their treatment of their indigenous peoples, the United States is still faltering at a full public apology.

Since 2004 there has been a resolution for apology before the joint houses. After years of committee re-writes it finally passed in 2009. Regrettably it was signed into law buried in the Defense Appropriations Bill[50].

Many Native Americans have met it with mixed criticisms and concerns. Often the complaint has been the lack of public announcement and recognition.

This is not to make light of the labor of love and efforts of those individuals, senators and congressmen who championed this apology. I, and others, are simply saying it has not gone far enough. Even though it has been signed into law, it was not publicly announced in any significant way[51]. This apology could be a wonderful first step, but such an important initiative like this should be spoken on national television by the highest authorities in the land.

In this regard America or its churches aren't providing the example. I was told personally by one of the remaining Powhatan Chiefs that in 2006 the Queen of England actually brought a personal and national apology to the remaining Powhatan

---

[50] See: Wall Street Journal Website: McKinnon, John D. *U.S. Offers An Official Apology to Native Americans. Retrieved 9/23/2011 from* http://blogs.wsj.com/washwire/2009/12/22/us-offers-an-official-apology-to-native-americans/

[51] See: Capriccioso, Rob, *A sorry saga: Obama signs Native American apology resolution; fails to draw attention to it.* Indian Country Today, retrieved 9/23/2011 from: http://www.indianlaw.org/node/529

Nations. Canada's Prime Minister spent over an hour on prime time television on their major networks making a full apology. Lets hope that our government will follow this example—but as believers in Jesus we can't wait for the government—the love of God should compel us to lead the way.

Here is the full text of the apology pulled out from the appropriations bill.

APOLOGY TO NATIVE PEOPLES OF THE UNITED STATES
SEC. 8113
ACKNOWLEDGMENT AND APOLOGY

The United States, acting through Congress—

1. Recognizes the special legal and political relationship Indian tribes have with the United States and the solemn covenant with the land we share;

2. Commends and honors Native Peoples for the thousands of years that they have stewarded and protected this land;

3. Recognizes that there have been years of official depredations, ill-conceived policies, and the breaking of covenants by the Federal Government regarding Indian tribes;

4. Apologizes on behalf of the people of the United States to all Native Peoples for the many instances of violence, maltreatment, and neglect inflicted on Native Peoples by citizens of the United States;

5. Expresses its regret for the ramifications of former wrongs and its commitment to build on the positive relationships of the past and present to move toward a brighter future where all the people of this land live reconciled as brothers and sisters, and harmoniously steward and protect this land together;

6. Urges the President to acknowledge the wrongs of the United States against Indian tribes in the history of the United States in order to bring healing to this land; and

7. Commends the State governments that have begun reconciliation efforts with recognized Indian tribes located in their boundaries and encourages all State governments similarly to work toward reconciling relationships with Indian tribes within their boundaries.

DISCLAIMER

Nothing in this section—

1. Authorizes or supports any claim against the United States; or

2. Serves as a settlement of any claim against the United States.

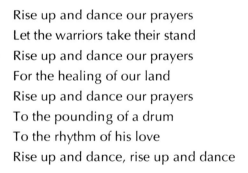

CHAPTER 13

RISE UP AND DANCE

Lyrics by Terry M. Wildman

The hand of the Creator
Is on the people of this land
Restoring hope and freedom
To help the warriors make their stand
The lies that have been spoken
To rob our pride and dignity
Were not the words of Jesus
He suffered shame to set us free

Rise up and dance our prayers
Let the warriors take their stand
Rise up and dance our prayers
For the healing of our land
Rise up and dance our prayers
To the pounding of a drum
To the rhythm of his love
Rise up and dance, rise up and dance

The Father's heart is beating
Like the pounding of a drum
The rhythms of his mercy
The heartbeat of his love
We'll take our stand together
In the circle of his life
We'll love each other
We will walk in the light

145

CHAPTER 14

RESTORING INHERITANCE

*I believe we are here today not because of the benevolence
of a controlling government, but because
the Creator has willed it to be so.*
— *Warren Petoskey, Odawa-Lakota*[52]

Dancing My Dreams

Native Americans have lived like refugees in a land that was originally theirs. They have been treated like foreigners and have been oppressed for four hundred years. A remnant of them have survived an american holocaust leaving them disenfranchised and broken—a shadow of their former selves.

A new friend of mine, Warren Petoskey, an Elder and Spiritual Leader among the Odawa and Lakota Nations is a strong believer in the Jesus Way. The town of Petoskey in northern lower Michigan was named after his great-great-grandfather—Ignatius Petoskey. His own father was a victim of residential boarding schools. Warren has spent more than a decade counseling and helping Natives who are suffering the residual effects of the historical trauma created by the US Indian boarding school system. In his book *Dancing My Dream* he laments.

> We, Indian people—those of us alive today—have survived
> five centuries of near-constant assassination and
> extermination attempts. We have survived genocide,

---

chemical and germ warfare, terrorism, sterilization, relocation, reservations, urbanization, boarding schools, orphanages and the foster care system, all of which were designed to erase the consciousness of what it means to be an Indian in North America. Our hearts have been on the ground because of all these things...[53]

A God Given Inheritance

When one considers what the American Indian has endured and survived, it is not difficult to see the hand of Providence in their preservation. A remnant has survived. Why would God reserve this remnant of Indian Nations?

I propose it is because of his great love for them as a people and because he has invested in them an inheritance and a destiny. God gave every nation an inheritance, he determined their original boundary lines, and even chose the exact places they would live. He decided when and where he wanted them to be.

Remember the days of old; consider the years of many generations; ask your father, and he will show you, your elders, and they will tell you. When the Most High gave to the nations their inheritance, when he divided mankind, he fixed the borders of the peoples according to the number of the sons of God.

—Deuteronomy 32:7-8

---

[53] ibid.

From one man he made every nation of men, that they should inhabit the whole earth; and he determined the times set for them and the exact places where they should live.

—Acts 17:26 NIV

Every tribe in North America feels a deep sense of connection to a geographic place. When asked to give up their land the response was almost universal, *"How can we leave the place where our ancestors are buried? The Creator chose us to live here, who are you to say we cannot?"* Consider these passionate words from the mouth of Tecumseh.

> *Where today are the Pequot? Where are the Narragansett, the Mohican, the Pokanoket, and many other once powerful tribes of our people? They have vanished before the avarice and the oppression of the White Man, as snow before a summer sun. Will we let ourselves be destroyed in our turn without a struggle, give up our homes, our country bequeathed to us by the Great Spirit, the graves of our dead and everything that is dear to us? I know you will cry with me, NEVER NEVER!*
>
> *These lands are ours. No one has a right to remove us, because we were the first owners. The Great Spirit above has appointed this place for us, on which to light our fires, and here we will remain.*

Jesus didn't come to strip the Indian of his culture and way of life, he came to fulfill and complete it. He came to affirm the God given values within our cultures and to provide the way for them to be lived out. He infused Native cultures with aspects of his own nature and character and has apportioned them a purpose and destiny. This purpose and destiny is connected with the land that he placed them in first. It is through Jesus that this inheritance finds full and complete fulfillment.

Priests of the Land

God has always had an original purpose for the First Nations People of North America. The coming of the Europeans has not changed God's foundational purpose for them. Has he kept for himself a remnant of Native Americans, perhaps as a secret weapon against the schemes and plans of Satan?

As the original people, American Indians stand in a unique place of authority and calling regarding God's purposes here. Even as Melchizedek, an indigenous priest of the land, welcomed Abraham and blessed him, so the Native Americans can also stand in the position of that ancient priesthood and as priests of the land they can welcome and bless the Abrahamic revelation that finds its fullness in Jesus. This is important in understanding the protocols God expects, giving honor where honor is due (Romans 13:7).

Melchizedek was a king and a priest of the land where God sent Abraham. This ancient priesthood predated the Levitical priesthood, which was established later under the Law of Moses.

As a righteous representative of those who God had originally placed there, he welcomed Abraham into the land, and blessed him. He had the God given authority and right to do so (Hebrews 7: 1).

The book of Hebrews, in chapter seven, spends a significant amount of time explaining how the priesthood that Jesus holds is not Levitical but it is the priesthood in the order of Melchizedek, and that it is greater than the Levitical order.

Melchizedek was a foreshadowing or a type of the Messiah who would have an unending priesthood. Because Melchizedek had no Biblical genealogy, no record of when his life ended, he prefigured Jesus whose life literally never ends (Hebrews 7:3). This ancient priesthood is a universal priesthood, not limited to the Hebraic genealogy; it is likely the same kind of priesthood that Enoch, Job and other ancients functioned in.

It is quite surprising and remarkable to note that Scripture declares Melchizedek was greater than Abraham!

> See how great this man [Melchizedek] was to whom Abraham the patriarch gave a tenth of the spoils! ... This man ... received tithes from Abraham and blessed him who had the promises. It is beyond dispute that the inferior is blessed by the superior.
>
> —Hebrews 7:4,6,7

How is it that Melchizedek is superior to Abraham? Respected Evangelical author Don Richardson in his book *Eternity in Their Hearts* gives a plausible explanation.

> How can we make sense of the Biblical claim that Melchizedek was greater in spiritual rank than Abraham? What was it that made Melchizedek greater?
>
> It seems to this writer that the answer lies in what Melchizedek represented, vis-a-vis, what Abraham represented in God's economy. The thesis of this book is that Melchizedek stood in the Valley of Shaveh as a figurehead or type of God's **general** revelation to mankind, and that Abraham represented God's covenant based, cannon-recorded **special** revelation to mankind. God's

general revelation is greater than His special revelation in the following two ways: It is older, and it influences 100 percent of mankind (Psalm 19) instead of just a small percentage!

Not that Melchizedek's prior presence in Canaan detracted in any way from Abraham's God given destiny.[54]

I propose that those Native Americans who, like Melchizedek, believe in the Most High God, stand in this place of *"general revelation."* They carry a similar spiritual authority in this land to that which Melchizedek held in Canaan. They have the authority to bless the Abrahamic revelation that finds its fullness in Jesus the Messiah; who is the inheritor of the promises made to Abraham as his offspring (Galatians 3:16). Like Melchizedek they can welcome and bless those who carry this *"special revelation,"*—the Gospel of Jesus.

In the Genesis story (Genesis 14:17-24) Melchizedek and Abram refer to God with differing titles and names. Melchizedek calls God "El Elyon" which is translated as "God Most High" while Abram refers to God as "Yahweh," translated as "LORD." But Abram recognizes that this indigenous priest believes in and represents the same God! Abram declares to the king of Sodom, *"I have lifted my hand to the LORD [Yahweh], God Most High [El Elyon], Possessor of heaven and earth."*

Don Richardson, in the same book, expands on this idea.[55]

---

[54] Richardson, Don, *Eternity in Their Hearts-Revised*, (Ventura: Regal Books/Gospel Light (1981), 31.
[55] ibid. 31,32.

They [Abram and Melchizedek] were brothers in El Elyon/Yahweh and allies in His cause! Since general revelation and special revelation both spring from El Elyon/Yahweh, it was to be expected that Melchizedek would share bread and wine with Abram and that Abram would "pay the tithe" to Melchizedek.

The amazing thing is that they have continued to do just that down through the subsequent history of mankind. For as Yahweh's special revelation—let's call it the Abraham factor—has continued to reach into the world through the Old and New Testament eras, it has continually found that Yahweh's general revelation—lets call it the Melchizedek factor—is already on the scene, bringing out the bread, the wine, and the blessings of welcome!

In America, I believe it is the Native Americans who are the "Melchizedek factor."

A Heavenly Download

In 2006 I was asked to be a speaker at a meeting in Sedona Arizona. The Glory Zone Ministry, led by David and Stephanie Herzog, was hosting a conference during Passover week called "Taking Your Inheritance". There were many Navajos and other Natives in attendance.

The night before, as I was going to bed, I was praying about the message I would bring. I remember asking God, "What is the inheritance of the Native Americans?" That night I received what I can only call a "download from heaven" in a dream. God was revealing to me all the scriptures from Genesis and Hebrews relating to Melchizedek and connecting it to the inheritance of the

Native Americans—as priests of the land. I awoke excited and told Darlene all about it. I had read Don Richardson's book and this seemed like a confirmation of this revelation through my dream.

So I taught this message on the last night of the conference. At the conclusion of the message I asked the Natives, those who would be willing to stand in this authority, to come to the front and forgive and bless those of European decent who brought the Gospel to them—even though it was misrepresented. We had the Natives hold the offering baskets to receive an offering to be given to the local Apache tribe. The Natives would represent the ancient Melchizedek order of priests blessing the Abrahamic revelation brought full circle in Jesus.

Even though many Natives are usually quiet and laid back, this was not the case that night! They rushed to the front and passionately began to speak blessings to those who were bringing the offering. The entire room seemed to explode with fervor and the atmosphere was charged with spiritual fire. The often stoic Native faces were bursting with emotion and tears, voices rose to a crescendo in the room. There were many spontaneous expressions of repentance and sorrow. This went on for at least half an hour as the Natives released forgiveness and blessing.

When the offering was counted nearly four thousand dollars was collected! And this was the last of several offerings collected that weekend. The offering was later given to the local Yavapai—Apache tribe by David Herzog's Ministry. The Tribal Chairman was amazed, because no Christian ministry had ever given a blessing like this. The money was used for much needed help for the Tribal Youth Center.

I believe that meeting was pivotal for the area of Sedona. Several Natives in attendance that night have since then moved out into powerful ministry. Many have told us that this affected the spiritual atmosphere of the region in a positive way. The Glory Zone Ministry has continued to bless and connect with the local Yavapai—Apache tribe since that time.

Who Are These?

As we witnessed this God reminded me of something that had happened a couple of years earlier in Montana. In 2004 I was teaching at a predominately white church there. After I spoke about the Native Americans and the need for healing and reconciliation I invited those who felt called to participate to stand. A handful of people stood and then came to the front for prayer. One lady was shaking and weeping and could hardly talk. She was obviously being deeply touched by God's Spirit. When she finally was able to compose herself she said that she had just received a powerful vision. She told me she saw what looked like thousands of white eagles all standing together. In the vision she began to move closer to them and discovered that they weren't eagles but they were Native Americans wearing white eagle garments. She could see the faces of the men behind the beaks and feathers. The voice of God spoke and said, *"Who are these?"* She had no idea and responded, *"You know Lord."* The voice spoke again and said, *"These are the priests of the land."* She felt an overwhelming sense of awe and respect for these priests—and the great need the land had for them.

Native Americans, who believe in the Most High God, can and should be considered to be "priests of the land" because of the unique place they hold as those the Creator sent here first.

This in no way is intended to imply that they don't need Jesus or that they supersede his priesthood in any way—or the priesthood of a believer in Jesus. Like Melchizedek they are an ancient representative and type of his eternal and universal priesthood.

I believe that recognizing and helping Native Americans to be restored to their place of unique authority and blessing is crucial to seeing God's full purposes accomplished here.

America desperately needs its Native Peoples!

Healing the Land

There are strongholds in this land and in its churches that relate, sometimes directly and sometimes indirectly, to Native Americans and the treaties and covenants that were made with them—and broken. These strongholds can only be broken in concert and cooperation with them.

Could this be the reason that our 24-hour prayer houses haven't yet brought revival? Is it because something needs to happen first? Could it be that the united prayer has begun to remove the scales from the eyes of the church in America? As we have already considered earlier, the giants of this land, Materialism, Greed, Abortion (which is the shedding of innocent blood), Divorce and more; all relate to the sins committed at the birth of this nation.

> *Every civilization carries the seeds of its own destruction, and the same cycle shows in them all.*
> —*Mark Twain*

I believe that one of the root issues that hinders the healing of our land relates to the Native Americans and to their relationship to the Euro-Americans who colonized this land and founded it on bloodshed and broken treaties.

How terrible it will be for the nation that kills people to build a city, that wrongs others to start a town.

—*Habakkuk 2:12 NCV*

What if God wants us to return to his original purposes for this land and its original inhabitants? Has justice and righteousness truly been for all? Could Christians today be seeking an incomplete inheritance, one that bypasses the original people? What if experiencing the full purposes of God for the church in America is dependent on helping the original people of the land come into their inheritance.

Many times we focus on our individual inheritance; but we forget that it is tied to God's righteousness and justice. The Nations are his inheritance.

Prophetically God speaks to his Son, the Messiah.

Ask of me, and I will make the nations your inheritance, the ends of the earth your possession.

—*Psalm 2:8 NIV*

Followers of Jesus share in his inheritance (Romans 8:17). He blesses believers so they can bless others even as Abraham was blessed to be a blessing to all the families of the earth.

The Native American Nations are a portion of the inheritance of Jesus and necessary in his purposes for this land and are deeply loved by him. Since he put them here first, it is possible that those who were first in this land have become last so that now the last will be first again. God uses those that are considered to be weak to confound the strong (1 Corinthians 1:27).

God's purposes always come full circle. I have observed that whenever there is great inequality God always works to bring things into balance—that is his justice at work. This justice leads us to the importance of reconciliation. Listen to the words of Jesus as he speaks about reconciliation, especially in light of America's injustices.

> So if you are offering your gift at the altar and there remember that your brother has something against you, leave your gift there before the altar and go. First be reconciled to your brother, and then come and offer your gift. **Come to terms quickly with your accuser while you are going with him to court, lest your accuser hand you over to the judge,** and the judge to the guard, and you be put in prison. Truly, I say to you, you will never get out until you have paid the last penny. (Emphasis added)
>
> —Matthew 5:23

Could there be an application of this for America and her churches? In the court of God's justice where do we stand in relationship to the Native Americans? How important is it to "come to terms" with them—to find a place of reconciliation?

A Corporate Perspective

Some have said to me, "Oh that's all under the blood! Jesus has forgiven us of all our sins, God won't hold us accountable." It is true that the blood of Jesus washes away all our sins on a personal level. However we are looking at this on a corporate level—community sin, national sin. Even so, the forgiveness of Jesus and the cleansing of his blood doesn't necessarily free us of the temporal consequences of our sins. God will forgive a repentant murderer, but that doesn't mean he won't go to jail, and face consequences during his earthly existence.

There has been a corporate arrogance toward the Native Americans, a belief that, *"might makes right"* and that *"the end justifies the means."* Even the Bible has been misused by taking Old Testament passages out of context to under gird the deception of manifest destiny.

Lets lay the axe to the root of these lies, come to terms with the past, and begin to move forward to a better future by doing the hard work of peacemaking that leads to reconciliation.

CHAPTER 15

PLANTING SEEDS
FOR A NEW HARVEST

Sow for yourselves righteousness; reap steadfast love; break up your fallow ground, for it is the time to seek the LORD that he may come and rain righteousness upon you.

__Hosea 10:12

And a harvest of righteousness is sown in peace by those who make peace.

—James 3:18

Those who sow in tears shall reap with shouts of joy! He who goes out weeping, bearing the seed for sowing, shall come home with shouts of joy, bringing his sheaves with him.

—Psalm 126:5-6

Preparing the Ground

The only way to get a harvest is to plant seeds. The process of seed time and harvest seems too slow to our impatient, fast food, cell phone, internet culture. Yet this is the Creator's plan for creation. Reconciliation begins with planting seeds.

If we are going to see a harvest of justice we must start at the beginning. To plant seeds that will grow the ground must be prepared. In Jesus' "Parable of the Sower" in Luke 8, he tells of those who plant seeds, good seeds, but get differing results. The results depend on the condition of the ground. In the parable it is people that represent the ground. The seed is the word of the

159

Kingdom of God—the message of God's righteousness and justice through his Son.

Often in our visits to churches we find that most people are so caught up in the busyness of life and the concern for making a living that there is little consideration for matters of justice unless it relates to them personally. Native Americans are very far removed from the mind and hearts of most people in this land. As in Jesus' parable the *"cares of this world"* choke the seed so that it doesn't produce (Mark 4:19).

Hearts must change, the fallow ground needs to be tilled. Fallow ground is land that is uncultivated, unplanted, dormant and barren. This is the condition of many hearts in America regarding the original peoples and any desire to see restoration come to them. This is one reason Darlene and I have been crisscrossing this nation. We are reminding churches everywhere of what has happened with the Natives of this land. Through our music and message we are attempting to prepare hearts for a significant harvest.

When we visit churches with our music and message we often find that most Pastors and leaders are ignorant concerning Native Americans and the true history regarding them. However we are beginning to see evidence of more open hearts, at times we see tears and expressions of shock and disbelief, we hear some say, *"We should do something about this!"*

Often after we leave, nothing is done. Remember, if we do nothing then nothing will change. Some will say, *"What can we do? Where do we start?"* Some take an "all or nothing" attitude, thinking the problem is too big, and has gone on to long—what's the use?

I heard a story about a young boy standing on the seashore where thousands of starfish had washed ashore. He began throwing them back into the ocean. A second boy came along and said, *"What's the use, there are too many of them, you can't possibly make a difference."* The first boy picked up another starfish and threw it in the water, and exclaimed *"made a difference to that one!"*

New Gatherings

What if we had gatherings and conferences that weren't about getting some new teaching or how to receive something from God, but to bless others—especially those who have been oppressed? What if we could find a way to make these gatherings a place where Indians might feel culturally welcome, one that puts their needs ahead of ours? What if Christians and church leaders could come together, not for ourselves, but to seek a process of peacemaking with our Indian brothers and sisters? What if the sins of the past and present could be acknowledged, owned up to, in a sincere and heartfelt way? What if acts of restitution could take place in these meetings where offerings would go to local tribal groups to help meet their needs?

Would this be a move toward what Jesus was talking about!

Could it be that God is tired of all our religious observances and wants us to reach out beyond ourselves and the limited witness that has been presented to the world? Is the church of America guilty of *"tithing mint and rue and every small herb but neglecting justice and the love of God"* (Luke 11:42)?

It's time to remember that our Indian neighbors have something against us. And, if we will be honest with ourselves, they have good grounds for it.

A Vision of Hope

Years ago, when we lived on the Hopi Indian Reservation my wife Darlene had a dream. In the dream we were in Flagstaff Arizona in the backyard of the leaders of the Youth With A Mission group that we were a part of at that time.

Darlene noticed that a dog was digging in the yard. She went over to where the dog was to look at the hole it was digging. As she looked in the hole she saw the face of a Native American under a sheet of ice. The ice was bubbling and beginning to melt when suddenly the person's eyes opened and blinked.

Darlene yelled, *"Call 911"* and the gate to the backyard burst open and a large yellow back hoe came in and started clearing the dirt away. When the backyard was cleared it revealed many bodies laying flat under a large sheet of ice—frozen. But as the sun began to shine on the ice it all began to bubble and melt. First one person stood up and then many followed. They were all Native Americans emerging into the warmth of the day. They were standing around rubbing their eyes and looking at one another. Then Darlene looked down and saw that there was another layer of people below them. As she looked deeper she saw ladders, and what looked like very old traditional people climbing up to the surface. She then looked beyond the backyard fence toward the mountain and saw how much dirt there was to remove and felt overwhelmed by the enormity of the task. Then a voice in the dream said, "Just take care of your own backyard."

We understood the meaning of the dream. The dirt represented all the years of injustice and the misrepresentation of the Gospel to the Natives. Our job was to clear away the dirt so that the light of Jesus (the sun) would melt the ice and bring restoration and salvation to them.

Peacemaking and reconciliation are a part of the process of removing the dirt so that, *"The true light that enlightens everyone"* (John 1:9) can melt the ice and warm the hearts.

In America, to see restoration, we have to start in our own backyard.

CHAPTER 16

PEACEMAKING AND RECONCILIATION

But the wisdom from above is first pure, then peaceable, gentle, open to reason, full of mercy and good fruits, impartial and sincere. And a harvest of righteousness is sown in peace by those who make peace.

—James 3:17-18

Reconciliation Roots

What is reconciliation from God's perspective? It is, first of all, an outflow of the love of God. God so loves the world that he gave his Son who would be the one who reconciles mankind to himself, and mankind to mankind. Reconciliation begins with the love of God and extends out into human relationships and people groups. It is through Jesus that Jews and Gentiles, perhaps the most segregated of peoples; find common ground and a reason to reconcile.

> *For he himself is our peace, who has made us both one and has broken down in his flesh the dividing wall of hostility by abolishing the law of commandments expressed in ordinances, that he might create in himself one new man in place of the two, so making peace, and might reconcile us both to God in one body through the cross, thereby killing the hostility.*
>
> *—Ephesians 2:14-16*

The primary purpose of the Cross is to reconcile man to God, but the overflow of this powerful and loving act also extends out into all relationships. The fall of mankind produced broken relationships, mankind with God, Cain with Abel, and finally nation rising against nation. The reconciliation Jesus secured reverses this curse and restores all relationships through faith in him. Reconciliation then, is the putting to death of all hostility through the love of God that is revealed in the gift of his Son to the world. This is what frees us to come into loving relationships with one another.

Why is it important to see reconciliation take place with the Indigenous peoples of America? First of all, it helps us participate in the love of God for all people. Secondly, it is through this love that God's justice and righteousness are extended to others (Psalm 89:14). Through all of this, reconciliation witnesses to the truth about who Jesus is and why he came into the world.

Jesus taught us that reconciliation between people takes precedent over religious observance.

> So if you are offering your gift at the altar and there remember that your brother has something against you, leave your gift there before the altar and go. First be reconciled to your brother, and then come and offer your gift.
>
> —Matthew 5:23-24

In America today Christians are very busy with church going activities. Christian conferences abound in this nation attracting thousands to come and learn how to receive some kind of new blessing. It could be to learn something new about the end times, how to financially prosper, how to grow your church, build your ministry, and a myriad of other topics. All across this land Christians bring their gift to the alter on Sunday mornings with a desire to please God. But what has been forgotten is that many of our Indian peoples hold some things against us—against the dominant society and their religion. Whether any feel this is justified or not, Jesus taught us to make reconciliation a priority over our religious observances.

The Road to Peace

Reconciliation is not just an event—It is a process. That process is the journey of peacemaking. Reconciliation is multidimensional; it is between mankind and God and between mankind and mankind.[56] It is those who have experienced reconciliation to God through his Son who should be the catalysts for reconciliation between individuals and people groups. Those who have experienced love and reconciliation with God are then able to freely give this to others. *"Freely you have received, freely give"* (Matthew 10:8 NIV).

Reconciliation is the restoring of a relationship that has been torn apart. Without the restoration of relationship there is no real reconciliation. Many have witnessed what is sometimes called "platform reconciliation" where a Native and non-native have stood on a stage and the non-native has expressed sorrow and asked forgiveness for what the white-man has done. Often the two people involved go their own way without any further relationship. Someone will then declare that the Navajo or

---

[56] I would like to acknowledge and thank Rick Love and Peace Catalyst International for ideas gleaned from the seminar in January of 2011 in Gibert AZ. Website: http://www.peace-catalyst.net/training/peacemaking-seminar

Cherokee, or whatever tribe the person belonged to, is now reconciled.

I believe reconciliation must go much deeper. Can you imagine a husband and wife who have been through a long and hard separation saying they are sorry to each other in front of witnesses and then go their separate ways—saying they are reconciled? They may be able to forgive one another but reconciliation requires a restoration of friendship and relationship again.

Beyond I'm Sorry

A while back I met with a Christian leader on the subject of reconciliation with the local Indian tribe. He facilitated a council of leaders for many churches in the region. As we began the meeting he asked me. "How many times do we have to say we're sorry?" My first response to him was to ask, "How many times have you said you're sorry, and who did you say it to?"

The truth is that in most communities there has been no significant effort to connect with the local Native American community, let alone to begin the process of reconciliation. In some places there have been attempts by small groups to make a public apology, but this usually doesn't include any ongoing relationships—nothing really changes. Reconciliation has to go beyond apology, beyond "I'm sorry"; these are necessary first steps in the journey, but there are many more involved.

I have noticed a tendency among Christian groups today, to try to approach repentance like a checklist. After becoming aware of the issues with the Indians and the US they often add them to the list and try to orchestrate a quick apology. Often these efforts are met with a mediocre response from pastors and leaders. It would be better to wait on God's timing, let him prepare hearts, rather than hurry the process. God is looking at the motivation of our hearts not just that we complete a checklist of repentance so we can have revival.

Peacemaking or Peacekeeping?

Peacemaking is the process that should culminate in reconciliation. Today some people confuse peacemaking with peacekeeping. Peacekeeping has been defined as *"the active maintenance of a truce between nations or communities, especially by an international military force"*. A truce is a temporary cessation of fighting or hostilities. Peacekeeping is a peace that is, many times, enforced on groups of people in hopes that peace talks can take place. Sometimes a truce is called, not to end hostilities, but to suspend them for a special occasion like a holiday.

Much of the US Government's relationship with the Indians has been that of an enforced peacekeeping. Few of the issues that cause division have ever been resolved, so there is only a semblance of peace. This kind of "peace" doesn't represent the love of God or the Gospel of Jesus. God hates this facade of peace.

The prophet Jeremiah's words to Israel confirm this.

> *They have healed the wound of my people lightly, saying, 'Peace, peace,' when there is no peace.*
>
> *—Jeremiah 8:11*

A Stumbling Block from Within

In my experience one of the greatest obstacles we face as we try to move toward reconciliation is the fact that churches and

Christian leaders are often not reconciled to each other. Much of the division between churches today is a reflection of the division that exists between peoples in this land. Sunday morning church has been called the most segregated time and place in America. This uncovers a deeper problem in our religious institutions—if we can't find ways to work together as Christians and see restoration between believers and church organizations, how will we ever reach out to others?

However, I do see hope as denominational walls are beginning to come down. In some places the churches and pastors of a city are working together. Sadly this is not yet the standard but the exception. Regardless we have to press on toward the goal.

The Ability to Respond

Jesus said, *"Blessed are the peacemakers..."* (Matthew 5:9). As followers of Jesus we have the commission to labor for real peace. If society at large isn't taking responsibility that doesn't mean we have to follow suite.

My understanding of responsibility is not based on a requirement of duty but on "the ability to respond". Peacemakers are those who have received peace from God who are then able to work toward peace and respond to the need for peace whether it is individually or corporately. As discussed in the first chapter of this book the Kingdom of God is a threefold cord, *"Righteousness (which is justice), peace and joy in the Holy Spirit"* (Romans 14:17). Wherever we find injustice we are faced with an opportunity to respond from the perspective of the Kingdom of God empowered by the Holy Spirit.

Restorative Justice

Since the goal of peacemaking is reconciliation it doesn't ignore justice, or take a neutral position, but rather it puts justice in the light of restoration rather than retribution or punishment. This is the kind of justice that God's kingdom promotes. It seeks the restoration of both the victim and the perpetrator—recognizing that the perpetrator needs rehabilitation. The path of freedom for the perpetrator is to acknowledge the wrong that has been done and bring restitution where possible. This kind of restorative justice has brought much healing in Africa and to the Apartheid conflict there.

Archbishop Desmond Tutu gives a much-respected definition for restorative justice.

> We contend that there is another kind of justice, restorative justice, which has characteristics of traditional African jurisprudence. Here the central concern is not retribution or punishment but, in the spirit of ubuntu, the healing of breaches, the redressing of imbalances, the restoration of broken relationships. This kind of justice seeks to rehabilitate both victim and the perpetrator, who should be given the opportunity to be reintegrated into the community he or she has injured by his or her offense.
>
> This is a far more personal approach, which sees the offense as something that has happened to people and whose consequence is a rupture in relationships.

Thus we would claim that justice, restorative justice, is being served when efforts are being made to work for healing, for forgiveness and for reconciliation.[57]

Who Leads the Way?

For reconciliation to take place it requires empathy and understanding between people groups. I believe in America it is those who are of the dominant culture, the oppressor, who carry the greater responsibility and should make the initial effort. The church in America today is predominately made up of those who are part of the dominant culture. Those who claim the brightest light should be the ones who lead the way.

Restoring What Has Been Lost

The Hebrew concept of peace or "shalom" speaks of all aspects of social harmony, welfare, health and prosperity. So peacemaking seeks not only the ceasing of disharmony but the restoration of what has been lost. Native Americans, in some ways, are not unlike Israel of old—trapped, hidden and plundered, with no one to say, "Restore!" (Isaiah 42:22)

Jesus came to restore what has been lost, not just to Israel but also to the Gentile Nations. The Gospel of Matthew confirms this as he declares that Jesus fulfills Isaiah's prophecy, *"I will put my Spirit upon him and he shall proclaim justice to the Gentiles… until he brings justice to victory; and in his name the Gentiles will hope."* (Matthew 12:18, 21)

Jesus reveals the Father's heart for all the nations of the world. He came first to *"The lost sheep of the House of Israel"*

---

[57] Tutu, Desmond. *No Future Without Forgiveness*. (New York: Random House, 1999), 54-55

(Matthew 15:24) and brought the hope of restoration—the Gospel, but after his resurrection he extends this to all nations, *"And he said to them, 'Go into all the world and proclaim the gospel to the whole creation'"* (Mark 16:15). The Apostle Paul later boldly declares, *"Or is God the God of Jews only? Is he not the God of Gentiles also? Yes, of Gentiles also..."* (Romans 3:29).

Why would we be surprised today that God would want to restore Native Americans? I propose that reconciliation must include a restoring of what has been lost, this includes the restoration of dignity, language, culture, land,[58] etc.

Is there room for this in America? Only if there is room in the hearts of God's people. Churches should become advocates for local tribes, proponents for the reclamation of land and resources to be returned wherever possible, using whatever influence is appropriate. Who else will fulfill Isaiah's ancient prophecy—for this land?

> *They shall build up the ancient ruins; they shall raise up the former devastations; they shall repair the ruined cities, the devastations of many generations.*
>
> —*Isaiah 61:4*

An End to Religion as a Weapon

He shall judge between the nations, and shall decide disputes for many peoples; and they shall beat their swords into plowshares, and their spears into pruning hooks; nation shall not lift up sword against nation, neither shall they learn war anymore.

—*Isaiah 2:4*

---

[58] I am not advocating that all land can be returned to the tribes. However there is much land that could be returned. Some tribes have large amounts of land, while others only minute portions. In some places local tribes could be given a place in the cities for a cultural center and gathering site.

Jesus paved the way by defeating, through the cross, the spiritual powers that hold the world in bondage. These spiritual powers use religion as a weapon for us to judge one another with. Religion has been one of the greatest causes of war and those who were advancing their religious beliefs and causes have spilled much blood.

He judges between nations and people groups by removing the reason for hostility. He does this by declaring that all peoples are the same, Jew or gentile, all fall short of God's original intention for them and are in need of his forgiveness and mercy.

He puts an end to religion as a weapon used to impose or enforce our laws and beliefs on others and grants all equal standing with him. Equal standing on the basis of his love and grace not on the grounds of following enforced religious rules and regulations. This is his peacemaking plan and the pattern for all who would be peacemakers.

> For he himself is our peace, who has made us both one and has broken down in his flesh the dividing wall of hostility by abolishing the law of commandments expressed in ordinances, that he might create in himself one new man in place of the two, so making peace, and might reconcile us both to God in one body through the cross, thereby killing the hostility.
>
> —Ephesians 2:14-16

Jesus is the Reason

Jesus himself becomes the reason for peace, and calls his followers to become peacemakers rather than judges (Romans 2:1). Those who are peacemakers have come to terms with their own propensity to judge, and choose rather to become those who bless. They understand the need to cooperate with God to bring his peace to those who are the victims of this world's judgments. Instead of judges and law enforcers they become protectors and deliverers. Jesus said that he did not come to judge the world but to save it (John 12:47). We, like him, are called to operate in the same spirit. For *"As he is so are we in the world"* (1 John 4:17).

> *The Spirit of the Lord is upon me, because he has anointed me to proclaim good news to the poor. He has sent me to proclaim liberty to the captives and recovering of sight to the blind, to set at liberty those who are oppressed, to proclaim the year of the Lord's favor.*
>
> *—Luke 4:18*

This is what it means to be a peacemaker—one who promotes the *shalom* of God. As those who follow in the footsteps of Jesus we continue his mission in this world—not through worldly weapons or strategies—not through political agendas— but through the empowering of his Spirit. Jesus said that peacemakers would be called *"sons of God"* (Matthew 5:9). They are sons of God reflecting the beauty and likeness of the Son of God as they continue in his footsteps.

Blessed are the peacemakers!

God's Kind of Praying

There are a growing number of 24-hour prayer houses being planted across this land but still revival tarries. Do the words of Isaiah to Israel (Isaiah 58) have an application to us today? They were wondering why God had not answered their prayers. Had they not humbled themselves? Had they not fasted?

Were they not delighting to know God's ways? His answer to them has a prophetic edge for today. I will take the liberty to paraphrase Isaiah's words.

> When you pray and fast it is really only to get something for yourselves. You are not caring for the oppressed and hurting. You are trying to get me to further your own agendas—to put yourself above others. This is not the kind of praying and fasting I am looking for. Listen to what I desire; find the oppressed and poor of the land and help them get back on their feet again. Share your food with those who are hungry and share your clothes with those who are in rags. Begin to pour yourselves out to others who are in need. Do not hide yourselves from your own flesh.
>
> —From Isaiah 58

Today Native Americans are, for the most part, hidden from the majority culture. Consigned long ago to reservations—to be hidden away from the sight of the public. It's time to stop *"hiding ourselves from our own flesh"*—and do for others what we would want done for ourselves. If we will do this, then God will respond in kind.

> ...Then shall your light rise in the darkness and your gloom be as the noonday. And the LORD will guide you continually and satisfy your desire in scorched places and make your bones strong; and you shall be like a watered garden, like a spring of water, whose waters do not fail.
>
> —Isaiah 58:10

He also says we will have a new reputation—repairers of the breach!

> *And your ancient ruins shall be rebuilt; you shall raise up the foundations of many generations; you shall be called the repairer of the breach, the restorer of streets to dwell in.*
>
> —*Isaiah 58:12*

The violence and bloodshed inflicted upon the original inhabitants has caused a great breach upon this land. Their villages and dwelling places lie in ruin. The ancient ruins in this land relate to the original people—they need to be restored. The relationship between the Native Americans and the Euro-Americans must be repaired.

God intended for the Europeans and Indians to come together in equality and respect; each sharing the strengths of our cultures with one another. In isolated places this proved successful, but overall this original purpose was ignored and aborted.

If we, as believers in Jesus want to see revival in this land; I believe it must begin by returning to this original purpose.

CHAPTER 17

RECONCILIATION AND CULTURE

Historically folks have approached Indians and wanted to carry out a program or something, and its always done the non-Indian way. If there's going to be any kind of reconciliation, it should done from the Native perspective. [59]
—John GrosVenor, Cherokee-Choctaw decent

Degrading Native Culture

America's colonists were self-assured of their superiority, intellectually and culturally. This developed into a kind of ethnocentrism that frequently caricatured the Indians as bloodthirsty savages with no sense of right or wrong. Native culture was often mocked and ridiculed. They were looked down on and treated like children that needed to be disciplined and put in their place.

Early missionaries among the Puritans, steeped in their own European culture, often acted out the same condescending attitudes. Indian spiritual beliefs were judged as pagan and simplistic. They concluded that the only way Indians could truly be converted was if they became civilized first[60]. That meant that Indians must become Puritans, in dress and language. In some cases Baptism was withheld until the Native candidate first dressed in civilized clothes, built a proper cabin, put up a fence and planted a garden.

---

[59] Two Rivers DVD, Greenleaf Street Productions,
http://www.tworiversfilm.com/index.htm
[60] Hiebert, Paul, Dr. *Anthropological Reflections on Missionalogical Issues.* (Grand Rapids, MI: Baker Books, 1994), 54,55

It was these Puritan Missionaries of New England that set the standard for future missions.

In the secular market pulp novels were written further reinforcing the negative stereotypes that had been developed. The Indian was characterized either as a savage or a romanticized tragic figure. In later generations movies made in Hollywood continued to infect the minds and hearts of millions of white Americans as Indians were further defamed and demeaned on the silver screen. This has only changed in the last twenty years where new movies have presented a more accurate account of this history. But the damage has already been done. Even today there are younger generations whose minds have been shaped by the stereotypes in these films. In my own extended family one of my young nephews once asked me, "So are you part Indian and part human?"

Where did he get the idea that Indians aren't human?

A Harvest of Mistrust

These historic seeds have produced, especially among Christians, a harvest of suspicion and mistrust of Native cultural practices, in particular spiritual practices. I have personally encountered Christians who automatically associate being an Indian to being a witch or a Satan worshiper. These Christians encourage and often demand Native believers in Jesus to renounce all aspects of their Indian heritage.

I personally know of two Indian friends, believers in Jesus, who were told by ministers to reject all their cultural ways. One was even told to renounce her Clan. Recently, when ministering in Michigan we met a young Native girl who was 8 years old.

She had visited a local church where the other children told her that she was a "devil worshiper," just because she is Native American.

The Bible never tells us to renounce our ethnic identities or our cultures. We can and should obviously renounce any forbidden practices, such as witchcraft or idolatry, which is found among all people groups. There is good and bad in every culture, and idolatry can disguise itself in many forms, including greed (Colossians 3:5).

A Common Misapplication

But, you might ask, I thought that, *"In Christ there is neither Jew nor Greek,"* doesn't that mean we should abandon our ethnicity? Actually it also says, *"there is neither male nor female"* in the same scripture passage (Galatians 3:28). I don't know of any Christians who would think we should renounce or abandon our sexual distinctions. On the contrary, scripture continues to make distinctions; husbands and wives, men and women, and Jews and Gentiles. It simply means that our bond in Jesus takes precedent over all these other distinctions—but it doesn't mean they don't exist nor that they should be denied.

Among some Christians in America there is a great debate over Native American culture. Some Natives are beginning to follow Jesus without abandoning their cultures.

Richard Twiss, a Lakota follower of Jesus, has been helping many to find new freedom in their faith for this. In his book *One Church Many Tribes* he brings some much needed insight.

Native culture, like all the cultures of man, reflects to some degree the attributes of our Creator Himself. It is in Christ

179

that we find the ultimate fulfillment of His holy and sovereign purpose for us as a people. If He has a unique role for us to play or a contribution for us to make in the fulfilling of His purposes for our nation in these days, then as the Church we must reconsider the place in the evangelical mainstream in America that we give to Native expression.

Yes, there does exist [in our Native cultures] *idolatrous and sinful practices that must be repented of; but the Word of God does not call us to turn away from being who God made us—Native people. When we come to Christ as First Nations people, Jesus does not ask us to abandon our sin-stained culture in order to embrace someone else's sin-stained culture.*[61]

Escaping Cultural Blindness

First Nations cultures and world-views have much to offer the church in America and the rest of the world. There is much, in their Greco-Roman influenced worldview, that blinds westernized Christians to portions of scripture. Everything is interpreted though this filter and grid. Someone from another worldview can offer insight and understanding of scripture that others are blinded to. The church of America needs its Native Peoples to help it break out of its culturally limited perspectives.

Often Native culture is judged by its peripheral beliefs and practices, rather than by its core values. In my own Ojibwe culture the central values are reflected in what is called the "7 Grandfather's Teachings". These are *Love, Respect, Wisdom, Honesty, Courage, Humility,* and *Truth.* Traditionally our

---

[61] Twiss,Richard.*One Church Many Tribes,*(Ventura,CA Regal Books), 78, 79

ceremonies were practiced as a reinforcement of these teachings. Other tribes share similar core beliefs. These ancient ways reflect the same values that Jesus taught. This is only one of many examples of the God given worth our Native cultures carry.

Reconciliation must also include repentance by those in the dominant society of the judgments that have been made against Native peoples and their cultures. Cultural expressions of dance and music should be encouraged and welcomed into churches.

Celebrating the Differences

God has created a great diversity in the Universe, his creation works together in unity. He created diverse colors, animals, plants and peoples. He made a difference between men and women—a reason to celebrate! Wouldn't the world be a dull place if everyone was the same? If everything was one color? If everyone had the same personality? God is the creator of diversity and has reflected this in nature and in human beings. This is true in cultures around the world; witnessed in music, paintings, and the like. We can have unity with diversity; it is the witness of Sacred Scripture and of all the creation around us.

This is the emphasis of our Seeking Common Ground meetings and our All Colors Together gatherings that we help facilitate. As we all learn to value the beauty that the Creator has blessed every tribe and tongue with we will taste the first-fruits of what is coming.

The Apostle John's vision of the New Jerusalem gives us a glimpse of this.

And I saw no temple in the city, for its temple is the Lord God the Almighty and the Lamb. And the city has no need of sun or moon to shine on it, for the glory of God gives it light, and its lamp is the Lamb. By its light will the nations walk, and the kings of the earth will bring their glory into it, and its gates will never be shut by day—and there will be no night there. They will bring into it the glory and the honor of the nations.

Revelation 21:22–26

I believe the *"glory and the honor of the nations"* that will be welcomed includes all the cultural expressions; the distinctive beauty of the language, music and art, that God has given every nation to reflect his glory.

A Higher Perspective

Years ago, when I first got involved in Native ministry, I remember attending a large mission conference. I was troubled that there was no Native American representation there. There were African style drums that were being used in worship. I remember seeing Asian drums, and other cultural instruments, but nothing from the people of this land. I complained in my heart to God, *"The Native Americans have been robbed!"* I inwardly protested. I will never forget what I believe was God's response to me, in my mind I heard a clear but quiet voice say, *"No, I have been robbed"*.

Suddenly I saw it from God's perspective. What a difference! Not just man, but God has been robbed, in his own church, of the beauty of Native American songs, dances and expressions of worship distinctive to them.

If we are going to see reconciliation then the dominant culture should humble itself and embrace Indians and their cultures, in ways that are meaningful to them.

CHAPTER 18
ALL COLORS TOGETHER

Lyrics by Terry M. Wildman

The color of skin makes no difference. What is good and just for one is good and just for the other, and the Great Spirit made all men brothers. I have a red skin, but my grandfather was a white man. What does it matter? It is not the color of the skin that makes me good or bad.

—*White Shield, Arikara Chief*

Color us blue, like the sky when it's new
Color us green, like the moss on a tree
Like the dirt on the ground, color us brown
Like leaves when they're old, color us gold

With a rainbow of beauty, and paint from above
Color us Great Father, shaded with love
Paint us people of honor, tinted with grace
All colors together, one sacred race

Color us red, with the blood Jesus shed
Color us pure, with hearts that are sure
Though our numbers be few, color us true
When the story is told, color us bold

CHAPTER 19
RESTORING ANCIENT GATES

They shall build up the ancient ruins; they shall raise up the former devastations; they shall repair the ruined cities, the devastations of many generations.

—Isaiah 61:4

Unexpected Guidance

In 2005 God gave my wife Darlene and I clear guidance to move from Arizona to Fort Wayne Indiana. It came though a vision Darlene received during a time of prayer. It was a clear vision that involved people we knew in the past that lived in Fort Wayne and the regional Indians.

One person in Darlene's vision was Ron Allen the pastor of Heartland Church. We moved to Fort Wayne in June 2006 and Heartland Church gave us a warm welcome. Heartland became our home church and when we weren't traveling we attended services there.

Another person in her vision was Dave Wilson who we hadn't seen in over 8 years. He was still living in Fort Wayne. He confirmed the vision and told us that he was raised on the Navajo Reservation where his mother was a teacher. Dave often gets "words" from God and functions in the gift of prophecy.

When we began to research the history of the area we discovered that Fort Wayne was a historic hotspot for relations between the Native Americans and the newly formed United States. The first major battles took place there because George Washington wanted to establish a fort at the junction of the three rivers, called Kekionga by the Miami Indians. Little Turtle, War

Chief of the Miami, said it was *"The glorious gate through which all the good words of our chiefs had to pass from the North to the South and from the East to the West"* It was a strategically important portage between the 3 rivers and the Wabash that led to the west. The Miami and 10 other tribes fought and won the first battles but eventually lost to General Anthony Wayne who established a fort there that was named after him—Fort Wayne.

In Greenville Ohio in 1795 the *Treaty of Greenville* was signed by the 10 tribes and the United States. Eventually that treaty and all the others were broken by the US and the Miami were placed on reservations. Then in the mid 1800s they were forcefully removed to Kansas and finally to Oklahoma. Those who remained lost all their tribal homelands and their federal status as an Indian tribe.

As we learned about this history we began to see the many layers of deprivation and injustice that had been suffered by the Miami Indians since the founding of the US. We were slowly beginning to feel the weight and magnitude of what it might take to see healing and restoration come. It became evident that the Lord had sent us here, to the place where it all began between the Indians and the United States of America. In a way, this place was ground zero for what was to come for all the tribes.

A Foundation of Prayer

Shortly after our move to Fort Wayne we connected with the Fort Wayne City Wide Intercessors, the Fort Wayne International House of Prayer, and Aglow International. These intercessors had been laying a foundation of intercessory prayer for the city and region. God had clearly shown these groups that there needed to be some kind of reconciliation with the local Indians. They had prayed desperately that God would send someone to help.

We began to meet regularly with these groups, sharing our ministry and experiences with Native Americans over the years.

One Small Step

The first breakthrough came at a special meeting at Heartland Church. Richard Twiss of Wiconi International, a ministry that helps Indians follow Jesus within their own cultures, was invited as the guest speaker and RainSong (Darlene and I) led the worship time. Word had gotten out about this meeting and it was packed out. Leaders from the Fort Wayne International House of Prayer were there along with people from other churches.

Miami Chief Brian Buchanan was invited and came to the meeting. He was presented a Pendleton blanket and when he stood to receive it he was welcomed with a thundering applause. Chief Buchanan later told us that this was an unexpected blessing and that he felt very honored by the warm welcome.

This was a good first step of peacemaking and none of us knew what should come next. Darlene and I continued traveling, for the next couple of years, sharing our music, storytelling and message abroad, as we all waited on the Creator for the next step. During this time we made a few friendships and connections with some of the Miami people in the area. We were introduced to one of the former Chief's of the Indiana Miami but didn't have any specific direction yet.

Honoring the Gatekeepers

Then in the fall of 2009 Ron Allen suggested we put together a several day gathering that would be led by Native Americans. He offered the use of Heartland Church's building for the event. This spurred us to begin planning, as we prayed together with the intercessors everything started to come into focus.

We would have a gathering to listen with open hearts to Native American leaders, and to the teaching of others who have paved the way in reconciliation. Chief Buchanan would be invited along with the Miami Council to come and share what is happening with the tribe. There would be an honoring ceremony, an acknowledgment from pastors in the city, and an offering would be received toward the Miami language camp as a step of restitution.

First I asked for a lunch meeting with Chief Buchanan to see if he felt this would be a good thing. He met with me and listened and agreed that this could be something very good. He said it was refreshing to try a spiritual approach instead of a political one. I gave him a copy of the DVD *Two Rivers* to show to the Miami Council (*Two Rivers* is a documentary of a reconciliation that took place in Washington State a few years ago[62]). Soon word came back that the Miami Council agreed to send representatives.

Then we began meeting with Pastors and leaders in the city and region. Soon there were many Pastors and leaders representing over 100 churches in the region agreeing to be involved. As word spread people started calling us from other states wanting to come and participate. The date for the gathering was set for January 29-31, 2010, and called "Restoring Ancient Gates, Seeking the Creator for a Regional Prophetic Awakening."

Confirmation

Soon after this someone brought to our attention a book called *Releasing the Prophetic Destiny of a Nation* by Dutch Sheets and Chuck Pierce. One of the prophecies for Indiana referred to meetings that would be led by Native American

---

[62] See: http://www.tworiversfilm.com/2riv_film.htm

leaders—which our gathering was being led by. The prophecy mentioned Christian powwows springing up over the land. It also stated that in Indiana, Native American drums would sound, breaking off the spirit of abortion.

We were all very excited about this word and the possibility that this meeting was fulfilling this prophecy. We had already planned to set up the room powwow style, in a big circle, and have a Native drum in the center to worship God—Indian style.

Soon, people connected with Chuck Pierce's ministry began to contact us and tell us they felt that we were fulfilling that prophecy. An Indiana prayer representative prophesied to us that this was the fulfillment and came to Fort Wayne to pray and counsel with us. Here are some excerpts from the book regarding Indiana[63] and the Indians.

> Are there some new beginnings for America that are…to begin in Indiana? Maybe Indiana is supposed to be a coat of many colors? Maybe you are a key to some things that have to do with healing a nation?
>
> Christian Native American Pow-wows going all over the nation…they were beating the drums…breaking the power of abortion off the nation. And a voice broke through the clouds and said, "Native Americans must lead this, African Americans must claim this. White Americans must lead this."
>
> I have shifted an authority in the nation, and I have come to this State to shift this authority.
>
> There are some new beginnings for America that are supposed to begin in Indiana.

---

[63] Sheets, Dutch and Pierce, Chuck D. *The Prophetic Destiny of a Nation*. (Shippensburg PA:Destiny Image Publishers, Inc., 2005), 207-211

Acknowledgement

A special plaque was made as a gift to the Miami Council. It said, "In Honor of the Miami People, the Original Gatekeepers of the 'Glorious Gate.'" A pastor in the area was selected on behalf of over one hundred churches in the region to present an acknowledgment to the Miami Chief and Council. I was asked to write the acknowledgment, which was agreed on with only minor changes. It was to be signed first by any pastors present and then by ministry leaders and witnesses.

The acknowledgment was as follows:

We, as pastors and spiritual leaders, representing a number of churches in Fort Wayne and the surrounding region, do corporately acknowledge our sins in relationship to the Miami peoples. We not only acknowledge the unjust acts against your peoples by our ancestors, but also our failure to act on your behalf, to publicly acknowledge or attempt to rectify those wrongs, in the generations that followed. In all of this we have corporately failed to represent a good witness to our faith in Jesus Christ.

We acknowledge the historical sins of our ancestors —

In the unjust acquisition of your ancestral homelands and the breaking of treaties and covenants;
In the forceful removal of your ancestors from their homeland and to bringing division and devastation to the many families represented;
In the dehumanizing of the Miami peoples and the cultural genocide that followed;

In the abuse of families and children by the removal of children to boarding schools that degraded their way of life and language.

Today we recognize and honor the authority and rights of the Miami peoples as the original gatekeepers and caretakers of this land. Even though we may differ in the beliefs and practices of our spiritual ways, we commit to respecting the Miami as a spiritual people who desire to honor the Creator of the world, who have a rich and beautiful cultural heritage, and a unique and important role in the healing of this land and the future well being of this city and region.

We realize that words will not make up for the wrongs done. So in the spirit of humility we now extend our hands in friendship to the Miami peoples in hope that we might begin a process that will allow us to walk forward to a better future for all our peoples.

Presented on January 30, 2010 at Kekionga—Fort Wayne Indiana.

A New Beginning

On Saturday morning a group of intercessors loaded into a van and drove to Greenville Ohio. This is the city where the treaty between the Native Americans and the US was signed by the Tribal leaders and Anthony Wayne. Their desire was to find the physical place where the treaty was signed and pray at that spot. Several people were involved including someone who carried Miami blood and had current connection with the tribe.

On the several hour journey, as they were praying, one person heard what they believed was God's voice say, *"When you get there speak to the rock"*. No one was sure what that meant. When they reached the site they found a plaque commemorating the treaty attached to a large rock. There, at the rock, they asked for forgiveness for all the pain and betrayal represented there and for healing and restoration.

On Saturday evening about 500 people were present at Heartland Church including many from the surrounding region and from over ten states. The room had been set up with the chairs forming a large circle in the center, powwow style. As RainSong led a time of worship, all began to move out into the circle and dance their prayers for the Miami Nation, joined by the Miami Chief and Council members.

It is hard to describe the feeling that was in the air that evening, it was like a river of liquid love was being poured out and we were all wallowing in it. Since then we have received countless testimonies from those who were there—all having difficulty finding the words to adequately express the experience.

It is nearly impossible to recount all that happened that evening but I'll share with you some of the highlights.

There wasn't a dry eye in the room when Harry Smith from Ireland knelt before the Miami Council and wept over the involvement of his Irish ancestors in the past.

An unexpected delegation came from Kansas, the place the Miami had first been removed to, and presented an apology and affirmations.

A local Muncie/Lenape Elder gifted the Chief with Wampum and Sweetgrass and reaffirmed the Lenape people's solidarity with the Miami.

An offering was received for the tribe, to be used for the Miami language reclamation efforts and other needs—about $2,600 was collected. We were told this was the largest single cash offering ever given to the Indiana Miami.

The Honoring Plaque was presented along with the acknowledgment that was signed by the pastors, leaders and witnesses present, then framed and given to Chief Buchanan and the Miami Council. A copy was also kept for the churches.

Chief Buchanan closed the gathering by reciting the Lord's Prayer in the Miami Language and declaring—*"Lets have a new beginning!"*

The following night there was a time of celebration; an evening of worship, dancing and singing—powwow style. A Lakota Chief, who had heard about the meetings and came to see what was happening, opened the time of dancing and celebration with a prayer in the Lakota language wearing his full headdress. We all thanked the Creator for all the amazing things he had done. We knew that this was only the beginning of what we hoped would become a lasting relationship.

A Quick Response

The next day Chief Buchanan sent a personal letter expressing his gratitude. Here is a small quote from that letter, shared with his permission.

> *The Compassion and Love shown towards my people by everyone was overwhelming in the most Noble way. Again, no words will ever capture this experience. On the drive home, it seemed like a dream that we were still living in. Today, it seems like a dream. I have spoke to those whom attended and ALL have said THANK YOU to me for inviting*

them to be a part of this. For those who were unable to make it, they will hopefully be able to gain some satisfaction from those whom did attend.

My people don't and haven't had the opportunity to enjoy this type of treatment nor have they ever experienced this kind of compassion from "People" in the community.

Chief Blue Jay, Brian Buchanan
Miami Nation of Indians of the State of Indiana

Looking back over the weekend we could see the fulfillment of the vision Darlene received 5 years earlier. All three men; Ron Allen, Ron Archer and Dave Wilson were there and participated in significant ways. And we believe the Indian in her vision was symbolic of the Miami Nation.

All came together right at the place where the three rivers meet at Riverside—to begin reconciliation at the Glorious Gate!

Walking the Path of Peacemaking

In the time following, much more has occurred between the Miami Nation and the Christian community in Fort Wayne.

A few weeks following the event, the Miami Council invited RainSong and pastors from Fort Wayne to their council meeting at their tribal center in Peru, Indiana. They presented us with a framed Certificate of Appreciation, signed by the Council, and members personally expressed their heartfelt gratitude.

The Associated Churches' council invited Chief Buchanan to come and share his heart with them. Later they took an offering of about $1000 for the Miami Nation.

The Powwow Committee welcomed us and other Christian leaders to their gathering that summer and had us enter the arena as honored dignitaries.

Heartland Church acquired a large drum and the Miami Chief and a Senior Council member came to help dedicate the drum at a naming ceremony.

The Miami Council invited the pastors and churches to join them in October of 2010 to participate in a grieving ceremony. This ceremony has been held yearly for the past 170 years to remember those Miami who were removed to Oklahoma. Chief Buchanan told the Associated Churches Council that no outsiders had ever been invited to participate. He emphasized the fact that if anyone would have been invited the churches would have been the LAST on the list; but now, because of the Restoring Ancient Gates gathering, they are the first. Pastors, ministry leaders and the Mayor of Peru Indiana attended it.

In the spring of 2011 Heartland Church hosted the New Beginnings Powwow and Spring Gathering. This event was made possible by the cooperation of members of the Christian community and the Miami Nation. It was considered by all who attended to be a great success and may become a yearly event.

RainSong was invited to open the Miami Nation Powwow in the summer of 2011 with a concert. We were well received and have been invited back for next year.

Through out this time friendships have been formed and grown between individuals. Small informal gatherings have occurred for the purpose of fellowship and the sharing of culture through drumming and arts and crafts. There has been ongoing reports of changed lives and new ministries being formed—all related to these small steps of peacemaking and reconciliation.

The story is not over. There is still much work to be done. Even though the Fort Wayne Journal Gazette followed up with a story called "Sins of History"[64], much of the community is still unaware of what has transpired.

We hope to make connection with the Miami Indians who were removed to Oklahoma. They are federally recognized and have a reservation with their own Tribal Council. We are praying and asking God to open the right doors to see reconciliation extend there also. Some progress has been made but it is sometimes a slow process.

Many people are still working and praying to see federal recognition restored to the Miami of Indiana. We would like to see land in the city of Fort Wayne returned to the Tribe; a place where they can have their own cultural center and opportunities for economic development. It seems, in light of the city's history it is the least that can be done.

---

[64] See: Rodriguez, Rosa-Salter. The Journal Gazette
http://www.journalgazette.net/apps/pbcs.dll/article?AID=/2010

CHAPTER 20

SEEKING COMMON GROUND

My friends, I have been asked to show you my heart, I am glad to have a chance to do so. I want the white people to understand my people… I believe much trouble would be saved if we opened our hearts more.

—Chief Joseph, Nez Perce

I have become all things to all people, that by all means I might save some. I do it all for the sake of the gospel, that I may share with them in its blessings.

—Paul, Tribe of Benjamin

Close to Home

Today, as I write this chapter, I am sitting in the Strait Gate House of Prayer in the town of Indian River located in the northern part of Michigan's lower peninsula. We have been traveling here and connecting with people in this area for the past 11 years. We have visited and shared at churches, houses of prayer, and homes in the surrounding area including Charlevoix, Petoskey and Indian River. The first-fruits of the seeds of peacemaking are beginning to show signs of fruit.

Darlene and I were both born and raised in Michigan, having grown up with very little knowledge of the Indian history of this State. The story of Indian relations with the settlers in this area is tragic. I will include two accounts, the first written by Andrew J. Blackbird, son of Chief Blackbird, and the US Interpreter at Harbor Springs Michigan, in the late 1800s.

Hidden in History

This narrative is from Andrew Blackbird's book *History of the Ottawa and Chippewa Indians of Michigan*. Here, in his own words, he tells of a holocaust experienced by his people through the deliberate introduction of smallpox by the British, during the French and Indian Wars in 1763.

This small pox was sold to them shut up in a tin box, with the strict injunction not to open the box on their way homeward, but only when they should reach their country; and that this box contained something that would do them great good, and their people! The foolish people believed really there was something in the box supernatural, that would do them great good.

Accordingly, after they reached home they opened the box; but behold there was another tin box inside, smaller. They took it cut and opened the second box, and behold, still there was another box inside of the second box, smaller yet. So they kept on this way till they came to a very small box, which was not more than an inch long; and when they opened the last one they found nothing but moldy particles in this last little box! They wondered very much what it was, and a great many closely inspected to try to find out what it meant.

But alas, alas! Pretty soon burst out a terrible sickness among them. The great Indian doctors themselves were taken sick and died. The tradition says it was indeed awful and terrible. Every one taken with it was sure to die. Lodge after lodge was totally vacated--nothing but the dead bodies lying here and there in their lodges--entire families being swept off with the ravages of this terrible disease.

The whole coast of Arbor Croche, or Waw-gaw-naw-ke-zee, where their principal village was situated, on the West shore of the peninsula near the Straits, which is said to have been a continuous village some fifteen or sixteen miles long and extending from what is now called Cross Village to Seven Mile Point (that is, seven miles from Little Traverse, now Harbor Springs), was entirely depopulated and laid waste.

Indian Point

Another account that is more recent in the area's history affects a small band of Indians who still live there. The following is from the website of the Burt Lake (Cheboiganing) Band of Ottawa and Chippewa.[65]

This place, once thoroughly Indian, was forcibly colonized a century ago in one of the most shameful and least-publicized episodes in Michigan history. There are no historical markers to tell the tale; only a series of unmarked white crosses on a bluff above the water along Chickagami Road, decorated with artificial flowers and sprigs of cedar.

This is the old St. Mary's Cemetery, the only remaining sign of a village that served as the social, religious and cultural center of the small Burt Lake Band of Ottawa and Chippewa Indians. These were no "backward savages;" they were hard-working Catholics who farmed, fished, and drew paychecks as lumberjacks and millwrights for local logging operations.

---

[65] Norton, Mike. *Indian/Colonial Point's Shameful Past* (Record-Eagle, 2000) Retrieved from http://www.burtlakeband.org/portal/?q=NortonHst/alias Used by Permission.

And this land was theirs, not by some vague aboriginal right or a promise from far-away Washington. They had bought and paid for it themselves under the white man's own laws. In 1836, the federal government had promised them a 1,000-acre reservation around Burt Lake; when it failed to deliver on that promise, the Indians pooled their money and bought Indian Point for themselves, deeding much of it to the state of Michigan in the belief that they were creating a tax-free reservation. Until John McGinn came along.

McGinn was a timber speculator with friends in high places, and he had his eye on the Point. Using loopholes in the state's land acquisition laws, he "bought" the land at an illegal tax sale in 1900, and a few days later—while most of the male villagers were in town getting their paychecks cashed—he moved in with Cheboygan County Sheriff Fred Ming.

Herding the women and children out into the cold autumn rain, they doused their houses with kerosene, set them on fire and ordered everyone off. The homeless Indians walked 35 miles in the rain to the mission settlement at Cross Village, the closest place where they could find shelter.

Three years passed before the state admitted the land had been taken from them through fraud, but it refused to restore their property; instead it offered them swampy property that wasn't suitable for farming. Eventually some of them moved a few miles north, to Indian Road, where a second St. Mary's Church was erected in 1908 around a settlement that came to be called Indiantown.

Sheriff Ming went on to become one of the area's big political success stories, enjoying a career in Lansing as both a state representative and a state senator.

Robbed of their land, the Burt Lake Band has been thwarted elsewhere, as well. Unlike other Michigan tribes, the small 650-member community has no revenue-generating casinos or high-priced Washington lobbyists. They've been fighting since the 1930s to win federal recognition for their existence as a tribe—a goal that has consistently eluded them.

"We're still here," says [then] tribal director Gary Shawa. "We haven't gone away."

Today "Indian Point" has been renamed "Colonial Point."

These two narratives are only a sampling of the many injustices that have been experienced in Michigan by the tribes. We have discovered that through the course of history very little, and usually nothing, has been done in local communities to even acknowledge, let alone rectify these wrongs.

A Small Beginning

Through the years of our visits here we have been able to connect with local believers in Jesus who have a deep burden to see something done. Through groups and churches like Freedom House of Charlevoix, 4 Fires Ministry, Petoskey House of Prayer, and Strait Gate House of Prayer at Indian River, we were able to begin a relationship with this small band of Indians.

In November of 2010 we helped facilitate a gathering at the Strait Gate House of Prayer that brought together pastors from eight area churches together with members of the Burt Lake Band, and others, including Warren Petoskey, a local tribal Elder and Kurt Chambers, the local Tribal Chairman. This gathering was called Seeking Common Ground.

RainSong led a time of singing and dancing with the help of Mike Peters of 4 Fires Ministries [66]based in Grand Rapids Michigan with a local branch in Charlevoix. During these meetings a local tribal member told the history of the area. Protocol gifts were given and Pastors and Spiritual Leaders were recognized and honored.

Tribal Chairman Kurt Chambers led participants out to the site where the village was burned out, where he told the story of what happened. Local Indian culture was explained and demonstrated during the meetings.

There was drumming, dancing, and praying in the Indian way. It was also a time of worship of Jesus and sharing of scripture. Together we all explored the common ground between the local Native beliefs and Christian beliefs.

As a result of these meetings a Council has been formed to continue moving forward in peacemaking and reconciliation. Members of the local Christian community have helped the tribe to start their own food pantry. One of the churches involved, Freedom House, invited Tribal Elder Warren Petoskey to speak at their church. Strait Gate House of Prayer has also had Native Leaders speak there.

There is more work to be done and there have been some small hurdles in this journey. A number of committed people are working together to see restoration come. As of the writing of this

[66] Kopenkoskey,Paul R. Grand Rapids Press. Retrieved 9/23/2011 from http://www.mlive.com/living/grand-rapids/index.ssf/2010/10/4_fires_ministries_reaches_out.html

book it has been almost a year since that first gathering. Those involved hope to see more churches and tribal members participating. Perhaps a formal acknowledgment from churches in the area could be presented to the local Tribal Councils. Other Tribal Bands in the area need to be included in this peacemaking initiative.

I share this as another example of the work it takes to see reconciliation. The labor of peacemaking is sometimes a slow progress but, if I read my Bible right, it is worth the effort. It is a labor of love.

Lets not despise the day of small beginnings! (Zechariah 4:10)

CHAPTER 21

BEAUTY FOR ASHES

To give them a beautiful headdress instead of ashes, the oil of gladness instead of mourning, the garment of praise instead of a faint spirit.

—*from Isaiah 61:3*

I could feel layers of the past being peeled away as we hugged not knowing what Creator was going to do next.

—*Michael Peters, Odawa*

An Invitation to Reconciliation

I would like to share another story of reconciliation with Native Americans happening in Grand Rapids Michigan.

In 2010 Mike Peters invited RainSong to bring our music and storytelling to a special event. Mike is an enrolled member of the Little Traverse Bay Band of Odawa Indians. He is the Ogimaw (Leader) of 4 Fires Ministry, in Grand Rapids; a church that reflects and honors Native culture and tradition as it teaches the message of Jesus.

In 2004 Mike was invited, along with other local tribal members, to be an integral part of a merger/reconciliation of the World Alliance of Reformed Churches and the Reformed Ecumenical Council into the World Communion of Reformed Churches. This merger was scheduled to be held in June 2010 at Calvin College in Grand Rapids. This gathering would represent 80 million Christians with delegates from 108 countries, and nearly 230 denominations worldwide.

Mike was asked to help facilitate a welcome between the delegates and the Indians of the Grand Rapids area of Michigan. As guests coming to the United States these representatives wanted to receive a welcome and be able to acknowledge the host people of the land, the Native Americans.

A Change of Agenda

In the beginning the planning meetings were focused on how the Native people would greet the 1000 delegates. But as the meetings progressed the tone and emphasis began to change. The planning committee realized that there had been no real reconciliation between the churches and the Indian community. This led to the development of healing and reconciliation workshops to be led by Native Americans throughout the 10-day event.

Mike began to share the beauty of Native culture with the leaders of the planning committee. He explained how he has redeemed the drum, the flute and praying with smoke into his own life and the practice of his local church's worship of God. The committee leaders responded with open hearts and even excitement. They invited Mike to participate with some of these cultural expressions in the workshops and events.

What had begun as a simple welcome was growing into a time of cultural exchange and a new understanding of the Indian history of the city. The opening ceremony was to include an exchange of gifts and Mike explained how tobacco would be gifted from tribal representatives to honor and welcome the delegates to the land. The church leaders were moved by this but wanted to know what kind of gift they should give in return.

As Mike pondered the answer he didn't realize that it would forever change the relationship between 80 million Reformed

Christians and the Native American Indians. Mike told the story of the past atrocities participated in by the Reformed Church against the Native peoples. If they really desired to heal and reconcile the past they should base their welcome on the following scripture.

> *He shall judge between the nations, and shall decide disputes for many peoples; and they shall beat their swords into plowshares, and their spears into pruning hooks; nation shall not lift up sword against nation, neither shall they learn war anymore.*
>
> —*Isaiah 2:4*

The leaders met this proposal with blank faces and a short silence followed by a request for another day to consider this. Mike left the meeting thinking that his idea had been shot down, but at peace in his heart for having proposed it.

The Healing Begins

At the opening ceremony there was excitement in the air as the Natives led a procession into the arena. Then came the protocol and gift-giving ceremony. After the church leaders had been presented with tobacco, one of the current presidents reached behind him and turned around with a sword in his hand that had been hammered and bent into what might be considered a "plowshare!" He presented this to one of the Native elders while acknowledging the past wrongs the Reformed Church had committed against the Native Americans. He then asked, on behalf of 80 million Reformed Christians, for forgiveness. He said that a new organization was being formed and they wanted to walk a new road with the Indian peoples.

Mike was overwhelmed with emotion and as tears filled his eyes he responded from his heart. Without hesitation he spontaneously took off his Native headdress and removed the replica of the peace medal gifted to his ancestor by President Franklin Pierce after the signing of a Michigan peace treaty. He walked to the microphone and gifted the church leaders with the peace medal. Mike explained that he could only represent his own family in this response, but wanted them to know he believed they spoke with good hearts, and that he wanted to walk the road of peace with them.

The arena burst into spontaneous applause and tears. Mike said that he could feel the layers of the past being peeled away as the leaders embraced him with a hug. As the day progressed delegates from the 108 countries came and hugged him and shared their stories. Non-native delegates greeted him with tears and heartfelt sorrow asking forgiveness for what their ancestors had done. One person even returned Indian artifacts that her father had found and apologized for taking them. The healing had begun! But what was Creator going to do next?

Later in a newspaper interview, Peter Borgdorff, the past president of the Reformed Ecumenical Council said of that Day.

> *I think in a real sense, it was an acknowledgment on our part in that history is spotted and painful, and we wanted to come to some kind of terms with that, so that it may lead to some kind of atonement. We are dealing with cultural genocide, and we wanted to find a meaningful way to that history and to the people that relate to that history. We are talking about various options [with Peters and others], but it's too early to know what form that future relationship may take.*

Walking the Road of Peace

Since that time Mike Peters has reported that the World Communion of Reformed Churches has followed through on their commitment. They are funding the building of a Native American community center in Grand Rapids. It will be a place of healing and reconciliation, where Native Americans can gather and be a community once again. It has been named *Aquene Nawayee;* "aquene" means "I am a friend, I come in peace" and "nawayee" means "center". It is a house of peace between the churches and the Natives; the English translation would be "The Friendship Center."

It is the tradition of the Annishinabe Michigan Indians, that one is to look ahead seven generations whenever making a decision. May this house of friendship and peace bear the fruit of the Kingdom of God for the next seven generations!

CHAPTER 22

PRACTICAL PEACEMAKING

As we travel we often find people who want to become involved in peacemaking and reconciliation in connection with the First Nations people. Here are a few practical ways to get involved.

For Those With Native Ancestry

Find out as much as you can about your Native American ancestry. To do this you need to interview the elders of your family or anyone who has ancestry information. Find out if there is a family member who kept a family tree often found in a family Bible. There are some websites on the internet that can help provide guidance; be careful not to pay for anything you can find for free on other sites.

If you know your Native ancestry do some research on what is the current location of your tribe today. Do they live on a reservation? Have they any land left? Where did they originally live? Research any treaties made with them and what is the current status of those treaties. Investigate the history of the area and find out if there has been any battles or massacres. Begin to prayerfully consider contacting leaders and members of your tribe and introduce yourself. Come with a humble attitude wanting to learn more.

Be aware that local Natives are sometimes leery of outsiders who want to say they are Indians. Some do not accept mix-bloods below a certain blood quantum. So don't try to enter into an argument about whether or not you belong to that tribe. Stay respectful and humble, admit your ignorance and appeal to them as someone wanting to learn more. Some Natives will be very accepting and willing to receive mix-bloods, especially those tribes who have very few full bloods left.

For All Who are Willing

People who have no Native ancestry can still be involved. Research the area where you live. Find out who the local Indian tribes are. Attend any of their powwows and gatherings that are open to the public. Never try to attend private gatherings without a personal invitation from a tribal member. Visit the vendors and buy lots of arts and crafts. Always be respectful of all the protocols and rules at powwows and gatherings. Never take pictures without permission; often the MC (Master of Ceremonies) will let you know when pictures can be taken. Don't touch people's outfits, which are called "regalia," not "costumes." A person wears a costume to pretend to be something they are not. Native regalia is worn to represent who we are as Native Americans.

Research the local area to find out if there have been any reconciliation efforts in the past or continuing efforts in the present. Join with those who genuinely want to see reconciliation and restoration. If you're a church member inform your church leaders of your desire to connect with Native people. Give them good books on Native Americans to help them prayerfully consider teaching and encouraging others to get involved.

Pastors and Churches

Pastors and church leaders should be leading the way by teaching on the value of reconciliation with the local tribes. What better witness is there to the love of Jesus in this generation toward the Native Americans?

There will be those under your care who will have a desire to be involved. Get behind them; support them with finances and up-front time on Sunday mornings. People will get involved with differing levels of participation. Appoint someone to be a representative for your church with the local Natives.

November is Native American Heritage Month[67], established by President George H. W. Bush in 1990. Every church in America should take time, especially in November, to pray corporately for Native Americans on Sunday mornings. Perhaps a local Tribal Chairman or Elder should be invited during that month to share the concerns of the local tribe during a Sunday service.

In 2010, President Obama designated the day after Thanksgiving as Native American Heritage Day.[68] This is the first time in the history of our nation that a day like this has been nationally observed. Unfortunately this is a difficult time to connect because so many families get together for the holidays. But many of the tribes are beginning to plan special events around that day and week. Get involved in whatever way is possible. With enough planning and preparation special events could be organized. After all, the very reason for this Holiday is the historic precedent of Indians and Pilgrims feasting together to give thanks to the Creator!

One step of restitution could be to take up an offering, at least once a year, to be given to the local tribe to help with their language reclamation camps and classes. Since churches in the past participated in the stripping away of Native languages, it makes sense that churches today would help Natives reclaim their

---

[67] See website: http://nativeamericanheritagemonth.gov/ 08/08/2011
[68] See website: http://www.whitehouse.gov/the-press-office/statement-president-native-american-heritage-day 08/08/2011

languages. After all, language is important to God—he is redeeming "People from every tribe and language" (Revelation 5:9).

There are many ways to make steps of restitution; it isn't an "all or nothing" situation. Churches and individuals can get involved with helping local tribes who are landless get land again. Sometimes city parks, county parks, or state lands could be returned. Farmers and landholders have occasionally returned land to the local tribes. A few years ago an individual citizen returned 150 acres of beautiful land in Indiana to the Miami Nation of Indians of Indiana.

Ask the local Tribal council about their needs; for prayer and for awareness of what can be done to help. A church group could get involved with an outreach—locally. But don't just come with your own ideas of how you want to help, find out what the needs are and cooperate with current tribal leadership efforts to bring restoration and help to tribal families.

Churches and Christians need to learn to share their faith in Jesus with more than words. The privilege of using words needs to be earned through respect and hard work.

>...Let your light shine before others, **so that they may see your good works** and give glory to your Father who is in heaven. (Emphasis added)
>
> —Matthew 5:16

Follow These Basic Guidelines

Don't be in a hurry! So many people are in too much of a hurry to "apologize" or make something happen. We have met people like this who often want to burst into powwows and make a "reconciliation" scene. Go slow; wait on God's timing. Pray and fast and get together with others who have a similar desire. Watch the "Two Rivers" DVD[69] and share it with others, then invite your church leaders and Pastors to do the same. But remember that every situation is unique, don't try to make it a formula, absorb and apply with wisdom what you are learning.

Get some outside help! Contact others who have been involved with peacemaking and reconciliation that have established good reputations. Perhaps your church would sponsor some of the Native Christian leaders to come and teach on Native culture and Christianity—but make sure they have a humble spirit. Some Native Christian leaders have been taught that all their culture is bad or evil and they can take judgmental attitudes toward local Native culture and offend tribal members.

Churches or community groups could provide a place in the community where Native people can be asked questions and heard. Small groups and talking circles could be formed that allow Native peoples to tell their stories with out any criticism or judgment.

Check out your own heart motives. Make sure that the desire for reconciliation isn't just a revival checklist item. Be committed to building true friendships and long-term relationships.

Government Officials

Mayors and City Council members, County Supervisors, Governors and other State Representatives and Congressmen, etc., can have an important role in facilitating reconciliation with Native peoples. Often the local levels of government are overlooked in this process. I propose that they may carry the greatest potential at a "grass roots" level.

---

[69] See website: http://www.tworiversfilm.com/2riv_dvd.htm 08/08/2011

Often there is land in cities and counties that could be returned to the local Indian tribe or tribes. City councils could invite and include a local Tribal representative to the council, not as a token presence, but in a real voting capacity. This would honor and value the place of authority that the Native tribes should be recognized for.

State Representatives, Congressmen and even local State and City officials often have knowledge about and access to funds that could be made available to the tribes in their jurisdiction. They could become advocates for federal recognition for those tribes seeking such. Sometimes money has been set aside to create some kind of memorial to remember famous Indian leaders. Instead of memorials to history, it would make more sense to use these monies for real restitution, perhaps a cultural center with powwow grounds could be funded—a living memorial! This might provide economic opportunities for local tribes, especially for those without federal status.

Media and the Press

Local newspapers, television stations and radio programs should be encouraged to feature articles and programing that will educate the public on the current status of the local tribes. Native American Heritage Month in November would be a great time to interview and feature stories about local Native People.

Often, controversial issues, such as casinos, sports mascots, and fishing rights are the only press stories released. It's time to give the Native Americans a public face that presents them in a positive light, instead of reinforcing stereotypes. Many local tribes have a unique understanding of the history of an area and can offer valuable insight and wisdom.

Get Involved

Let's not just talk about it, or relegate it to someone else; or rush blindly in and be in too much of a hurry—but if we continue to do nothing then nothing will change. There are opportunities at every level of society for people to get involved.

How about you?

PART 4

AMERICA'S PROPHETIC LANDSCAPE

My son, eat honey, for it is good, and the drippings of the honeycomb are sweet to your taste. Know that wisdom is such to your soul; if you find it, there will be a future, and your hope will not be cut off.

—Proverbs 24:13-14

The more you take responsibility for your past and present, the more you are able to create the future you seek.

—Author Unknown

We have the power to make this the best generation of mankind in the history of the world or to make it the last.

—John F. Kennedy

The future is something which everyone reaches at the rate of 60 minutes an hour, whatever he does, whoever he is.

—C. S. Lewis

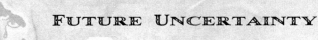

CHAPTER 23

FUTURE UNCERTAINTY

Conditional Prophecy

Prophecy isn't primarily seeing into the future. At its core, prophecy coveys the heart and mind of God for the present time. It may also predict events to come but this is usually to warn the hearers of the consequences of continuing on their present course; or it may be to bring guidance and encouragement. Prophecy is often, but not always, conditional; changed hearts and direction can alter the outcome. Consider the Word of God through the Prophet Jeremiah.

> *If at any time I declare concerning a nation or a kingdom, that I will pluck up and break down and destroy it, and if that nation, concerning which I have spoken, turns from its evil, I will relent of the disaster that I intended to do to it.*
>
> *—Jeremiah 18:7-8*

The book of Jonah also confirms this.

> *Then the word of the LORD came to Jonah the second time, saying, "Arise, go to Nineveh, that great city, and call out against it the message that I tell you." So Jonah arose and went to Nineveh, according to the word of the LORD. Now Nineveh was an exceedingly great city, three days' journey in breadth. Jonah began to go into the city, going a day's journey. And he called out, "Yet forty days, and Nineveh shall be overthrown!"*
>
> *—Jonah 1:1-4*

No conditions were stated in this announcement, just that in *"forty days Nineveh shall be overthrown."* The people of Nineveh responded with repentance, fasted and changed their ways. So God changed his mind.

> *When God saw what they did, how they turned from their evil way, God relented of the disaster that he had said he would do to them, and he did not do it.*
>
> —Jonah 3:10

Please note, it was when, *"God saw what they did"* that he changed his mind. If prayer, fasting and repentance is genuine it will be accompanied by a change in actions. What begins in a heartfelt sorrow and desire to see things change must result in acts of acknowledgement, restitution and restoration.

Back to the Future

I stand with those who believe that God still speaks today through modern prophets. Even so, there are a myriad of prophetic voices on the airwaves and the Internet that are presenting conflicting messages. It is difficult to sort through this prophetic confusion to discern what the heart of God is for the future of America. This is not surprising because ancient Israel and even the early church faced similar conditions.

Conflicting prophecies don't always mean that one is true and the other false. Sometimes prophetic people are seeing the differing pieces of the same puzzle, *"For we know in part and we prophesy in part"* (1 Corinthians 13:9). Another thing to be aware of is people often interpret what they are seeing or hearing through their own theological, doctrinal and cultural glasses.

To "see" the future we need to read the *"signs of the times"* accurately, with the help of the Holy Spirit. By viewing the present through the lens of the past we can then look to the future. Jesus and the New Testament writers often referred to conditions and examples in the past to make a point about the present and the future (See: Matthew 24:3-44, 2 Peter 2:5-9, 1 Corinthians 10:11).

In this book we have journeyed back to America's past to get a view of the future. We have had the aid of a Native American viewpoint to help set us free from our cultural blindness. We must compare America's past, with Biblical examples of other nations who behaved in similar ways. We can then consider their outcome to have a better understanding of the signs we see in the present, and what they may point to for the future.

In light of America's past, and the signs in the present, I am deeply troubled and concerned about the future of this nation. It appears that the seeds planted at its founding and the resulting harvests of injustice, point to even greater problems for the future.

An Ominous Portrait

At the present time, as a nation, the US is politically polarized and functionally gridlocked, with politicians pointing the finger of blame rather than seeking solutions. America is overfed yet malnourished, economically powerful but stymied with greed, technologically advanced in medicine, at the same time, in a medical crisis. It is the greatest superpower on earth, with no power to produce lasting peace. America is a nation that promotes infantile injustice—the killing of its unborn children. Infected with terrorism, national debt and greed, family breakdown, nationwide obesity, healthcare crisis, religious conflicts, language wars, gender confusion, aggressive sexual perversion, we face a harvest of unmanageable proportions.

America's churches seem to mirror the nation, sharing with it similar statistics. There are segregated congregations, overly stuffed with hearing God's Word but weak in doing it. Churches are often territorial and competitive; rich by worldly standards yet in God's eyes *"wretched, pitiable, poor, blind, and naked"* (Revelation 3:17). There is an epidemic of Christians who arrogantly bash our leaders and even demonize the Presidents. This casts shame on the name of Christ. Then there are extreme paranoid groups that claim the name Christian yet are militant militias, arming themselves to fight the Antichrist in some kind of self made Armageddon.

The current condition of the churches in America reveals that they too seem to be reaping the consequences of history, and appear to show little promise of the ability to morally or spiritually lead this nation into a path of repentance.

Hope for the Future

In spite of all of this I still believe there is hope for the future of America. Our Creator has already shown much patience and mercy toward this nation. I expect he will continue to do so. He does not want anyone to perish—but to wake up. God's judgments are also full of his mercy, forbearance and kindness— but we are warned not to presume on this (Romans 2:4).

Even though *"judgment is without mercy to one who has shown no mercy,"* the converse is that, *"mercy triumphs over judgment."* This means that God's judgment is merciful to those who have shown mercy (James 2:13).

Historically there have been those who treated the Indians justly, such as William Penn who kept a 70 year covenant with the Indians of Pennsylvania. And many others over the years who worked hard advocating for the tribes against the fierce tide of opposition. Even now there are peacemakers who are praying for and seeking reconciliation.

I am sure that God weighs all these things in the balance—he is a just God. There is still time to continue to act in mercy and kindness in bringing healing and restoration to those tribes who are still here. While "today" is still called "today" our hearts can be softened (Hebrews 3:13).

Even if America must come under God's judgment, and reap what it has sown, we must remember that judgment isn't punishment, it is for correction, to restore and bring balance again—to set things right. However, that process is often difficult to bear.

As Jesus' followers we must remember that God will begin his process of judgment with his churches, convicting and correcting them so they will not be judged with the world.

If we can learn to hear the voice of the Holy Spirit and follow his guidance, we need not fear the judgments of God. Some of the greatest signs and wonders ever experienced in Israel occurred during a time of judgment. When God poured out his greatest judgment on Egypt during the first Passover, those who followed his instructions were spared and eventually blessed.

A friend of mine, Shannon Vinsonhaler, comments on this in his book *Divine Times*.

> *Sin will always and must always be judged. For revival to come to Israel, the issue of sin had to be confronted.*[70]
>
> *When God is moving in judgment, He will also pour out his Spirit that will match or exceed the degree of*

[70] Vinsonhaler, Shannon, *Divine Times*. (Monahans, TX: Lindale Publications, 2009), 27.

judgment being poured out. If we are facing the greatest days of judgment ahead, then we are also facing the greatest outpouring of the Holy Spirit we have ever known.[71]

But what about our American freedoms? What if we lose those? The ones who are followers of Jesus are not dependent on the government for their freedom, anymore than the early followers of Jesus were dependent on Rome. Real freedom is a gift from God, not the government, *"For if the Son sets you free, you will be free indeed" (John 8:36).*

In the event that we, as believers in Jesus, find ourselves in a worse captivity in the future, to this government or to a foreign government, we will have to adapt to whatever condition we find ourselves in. We must learn to discern the voice of God and interpret the signs of the times.

Let us all learn from Israel of old, captive in Babylon, succumbing to the promises of false prophets, as God speaks a word of exhortation and comfort through Jeremiah.

> *But seek the welfare of the city where I have sent you into exile, and pray to the LORD on its behalf, for in its welfare you will find your welfare... For I know the plans I have for you, declares the LORD, plans for welfare and not for evil, to give you a future and a hope.*
>
> *—Jeremiah 29:7,11*

---

[71] ibid. p. 17

Final Words

I have presented the darker side of the history of America and its churches as a wakeup call—if you will—a sounding of the shofar! Anyone who has studied American Indian history knows that I could have painted an even darker picture—for the reality is worse than my telling.

In the opening of this book I retold the Biblical story of Israel and the Gibeonites. I believe this story illustrates the relationship between the United States of America and the Native Americans. This is not to say that I consider the United States as having any unique covenant with God as was the case of Israel. The similarity lies in the fact that the US made oaths and treaties with the Indians not unlike those made with the Gibeonites. The difference lies in the circumstances of the treaties. The US approached the Indians where in the Biblical story the Gibeonites approached Israel. The US often forced the treaties upon the Indians after defeating them in battle and time and again used treachery and deceit to ratify those covenants. A single treaty was made between the two nations in the Biblical story while the US made treaties with several hundred tribal nations.

Regardless of the similarities or differences this fact remains—God holds people and nations accountable to the covenants they have sworn themselves to. God held Israel answerable to the covenant with the Gibeonites—will he not do the same with America?

The historic and prophetic landscape of this nation should be considered in the light of the parable told by Matthew of the foolish and wise builders. Is America's foundation built upon the rock of *doing Jesus words*? Or is it built on the sand of *hearing his words but failing to do them*.

The second foundation will not support the house built upon it but will eventually succumb to the storms. It seems that this nation is heading for what some are calling "the perfect storm." Will America sink into the sand of a false foundation? And what of her churches?

And everyone who hears these words of mine and does not do them will be like a foolish man who built his house on the sand. And the rain fell, and the floods came, and the winds blew and beat against that house, and it fell, and great was the fall of it.

— *Matthew 7:26-27*

I leave you with this thought and prayer—may we all earnestly consider the **signs of the times,** recognize the **time of our visitation,** and do **the things that make for peace.**

Miigwech bizindawiyeg (Thank you for listening),

Terry M. Wildman
Gitchi-Animiki-Meno-Mashkiki-Manidoo
Voice of the Great Thunder with a Good Medicine Spirit

AFTERWORD

TWO OR THREE WITNESSES

*Let two or three prophets speak, and let the others
weigh what is said.*

—*1 Corinthians 14:29*

I present some of the words of Native American Elders and Chiefs for the reader to consider and weigh. Sometimes prophecy is simply declaring the heart of God. Here are a few words that in my opinion, are worth pondering.

You must speak straight so that your words may go as sunlight into our hearts. Speak Americans—I will not lie to you; do not lie to me.

—Cochise, Chiricahua Apache Chief

How smooth must be the language of the whites, when they can make right look like wrong, and wrong like right.

—Black Hawk, Sauk

Why should you take by force from us that which you can obtain by love? Why should you destroy us who have provided you with food? What can you get by war?

—King Wahunsonacook, Powhatan

I think that wherever the Great Spirit places his people, they ought to be satisfied to remain, and thankful for what he has given them, and not drive others from the country he has given them because it happens to be better than theirs!

—Black Hawk, Sauk

Your forefathers crossed the great water and landed on this island. Their numbers were small. We took pity on them and they sat down among us. We gave them corn and meat. They gave us poison in return.

—Sagoyewatha (Red Jacket), Seneca

They made us many promises, more than I can remember. But they kept but one, they promised to take our land—and they took it.

—Chief Red Cloud, Sioux

As a child, I understood how to give; I have forgotten that grace since I became civilized. I lived the natural life, whereas now I now live the artificial. Any pretty pebble was valuable then, every growing tree an object of reverence.

Now I worship with the white man before a painted landscape whose value is estimated in dollars! Thus the Indian is reconstructed, as the natural rocks are ground to powder and made into artificial blocks that may be built into the walls of modern society.

—Ohiyesa, Lakota

But in the long hundred years since the white man came, I have seen my freedom disappear like the salmon going mysteriously out to sea. The white man's strange customs which I could not understand, pressed down upon me until I could no longer breathe. When I fought to protect my land and my home, I was called a savage. When I neither understood nor welcomed this way of life, I was called lazy. When I tried to rule my people, I was stripped of my authority.

—Chief Dan George, Salish

The path to glory is rough, and many gloomy hours obscure it. May the Great Spirit shed light on your path, so that you may never experience the humility that the power of the American government has reduced me to. This is the wish of a man who, in his native forests, was once as proud and bold as yourself.

—Black Hawk, Sauk

"Civilization" has been thrust upon me since the days of the reservations, and it has not added one whit to my sense of justice, to my reverence for the rights of life, to my love for truth, honesty, and generosity, or to my faith in Wakan Tanka, God of the Lakotas.

—Chief Luther Standing Bear, Oglala Sioux

You now have become a great people, and we have scarcely a place left to spread our blankets. You have got our country now, but you are not satisfied. You want to force your religion upon us. We are told that you have been preaching to the white people in this place. These people are our neighbors. We will wait a little while, and see what effect your preaching has upon them. If we find it does them good, makes them honest and less disposed to cheat Indians, we will then consider again what you have said.

—Red Jacket, Seneca

Whenever the white man treats the Indian as they treat each other then we shall have no more wars. We shall be all alike— brothers of one father and mother, with one sky above us and one country around us and one government for all. Then the Great Spirit Chief who rules above will smile upon this land and send rain to wash out the bloody spots made by brothers' hands upon the face of the earth. For this time the Indian race is waiting and praying. I hope no more groans of wounded men and women will ever go to the ear of the Great Spirit Chief above, and that all people may be one people.

—Chief Joseph, Nez Perce

From Wakan Tanka, the Great Spirit, there came a great unifying life force that flowed in and through all things—the flowers of the plains, blowing winds, rocks, trees, birds, animals— and was the same force that had been breathed into the first man. Thus all things were kindred, and were brought together by the same Great Mystery.

—Chief Luther Standing Bear, Oglala Sioux

I cannot think that we are useless or God would not have created us. There is one God looking down on us all. We are all the children of one God. The sun, the darkness, the winds are all listening to what we have to say.

—Geronimo, Apache

I remember the old men of my village. These old, old men used to prophesy about the coming of the white man. They would go about tapping their canes on the adobe floor of the house, and call to us children.

"Listen! Listen! The gray-eyed people are coming nearer and nearer. They are building an iron road. They are coming nearer every day. There will be a time when you will mix with these people. That is when the Gray Eyes are going to get you drink hot, black water, which you will drink whenever you eat. Then your teeth will become soft."

"They will get you to smoke at a young age, so that your eyes will run tears on windy days, and your eyesight will be poor. Your joints will crack when you want to move slowly and softly."

"You will sleep on soft beds and will not like to rise early. When you begin to wear heavy clothes and sleep under heavy covers, then you will grow lazy. Then there will be no more singing heard in the valleys you walk."

"When you begin to eat with iron sticks, your tones will grow louder. You will speak louder and talk over your parents. You will grow disobedient, You will mix with those gray-eyed people, and you will learn their ways; you will break up your homes, and murder and steal."

Such things have come true, and I have to compare my generation with the old generation. We are not as good as they were; we are not as healthy as they were. How did these old men know what was coming? That is what I would like to know.

—James Paytiamo, Acoma Pueblo

ABOUT THE AUTHOR

Terry Wildman was born and raised in Western Michigan. He is of Ojibwe (Chippewa) and Yaqui ancestry. Terry is a recording artist and engineer, songwriter, storyteller, speaker, Bible teacher and now an author. This is his first book.

Terry is the "Chief" of Rain Ministries, a non-profit organization based in Arizona. Since the year 2000 as "RainSong" he and his wife Darlene have invested their lives sharing the message of Jesus with Native Americans. They have produced four music CD's, Sacred Warrior, Rising Sun, Rise Up and Dance and Hoop of Life. Their music style is a folk-rock blend with Native American instruments and melodies.

In 2004 RainSong was nominated for a Grammy award and two Nammy awards. In 2005 they won the "American Christian Music Award" for the category of "Favorite Band/Duo–Breakout".

In 2008 they were nominated for two Nammy Awards, one for "Best Song of the Year," All Colors Together, and for "Best Gospel Recording" for their CD Rise Up and Dance. Terry and Darlene were presenters that year at the awards ceremony held in Niagara Falls, New York.

They also produced a storytelling CD with a musical background called "The Great Story from the Sacred Book." This CD won the Nammy (Native American Music Award) for "Best Spoken Word" in 2009. They released a booklet to compliment the CD through Indian Life Ministries based in Manitoba, Canada, (http://www.indianlife.org).

In 2011 RainSong was recognized with another Nammy Award (along with other artists), for a flute song by Darlene on a compilation CD called "The Color of Hope."

> We are dedicating our time and the gifts Creator has given us to serve the First Nations People of North America. We are working and praying for reconciliation, with dignity and harmony restored to individuals, families, clans, and tribal nations.
>
> We believe that the message of Creator's Son Jesus is for all people and will transform the lives of all who follow him. But we also believe that the message must be embraced within the context of every culture to be effective.

Terry is available as a speaker for seminars, conferences, churches, and more. As RainSong, he and his wife Darlene bring Native American style original music to your powwow, gathering, church meeting or conference.

CONTACT INFORMATION

Email
signlanguage@rainsongmusic.com

Website
www.rainsongmusic.com

Sign Language Book Blog
www.signlanguagebook.wordpress.com

ABOUT THE COVER

Cover Art
The cover art is from a series of paintings called "Forgiveness" by the artist Kristen Lee Rahner. Used by Permission. The title of the painting is "Ground Breaking"

About the Artist
Kristen lives in Southern California. She can be reached at: barkeyes@sbcglobal.net and Kristen Lee Rahner Guzman on Facebook.

Cover Design
Mark Sequeira, MJA Studios designed the cover and the back of the book. You can contact Mark by email at mark@mjastudios.com.

Recommended Reading

One Church Many Tribes, by Richard Twiss (Lakota), Published by Regal Books, from Gospel Light, Ventura California, www.wiconi.com

Joshua in 3-D: A Commentary on Biblical Conquest and Manifest Destiny by Prof. L. Daniel Hawk, Published by Cascade Books, Eugene Oregon

Mixed Blood but Not Mixed Up, by Randy Woodley (Keetoowah Band Cherokee), Published by Eagle's Wings Ministry, www.eagleswingsministry.com

The Complete Idiots Guide to Native American History, by Prof. Walter C. Flemming (Kickapoo), Published by Alpha Penguin Group, USA

Eternity in Their Hearts, by Don Richardson, Published by Regal Books, from Gospel Light, Ventura California

The Earth Shall Weep, by James Wilson, Published by Grove Press, New York, NY

Remembering Jamestown: Hard Questions About Christian Mission, Edited by Amos Yong and Barbara Brown Zikmund, Published by Pickwick Publications, Eugene, OR

When the Mississippi Ran Backwards, by Jay Feldman, Published by Free Press, a division of Simon and Schuster, New York, NY

CPSIA information can be obtained at www.ICGtesting.com
Printed in the USA
BVOW032348180612

293007BV00003B/1/P